# THE UPSIDE OF TROUBLE

# THE UPSIDE OF TROUBLE

Anthony Shaw

Book Guild Publishing
Sussex, England

First published in Great Britain in 2005 by
The Book Guild Ltd
25 High Street
Lewes, East Sussex
BN7 2LU

Typesetting in Times by
Keyboard Services, Luton, Bedfordshire

Printed in Great Britain by
CPI Bath

A catalogue record for this book is available from the
British Library

ISBN 1 85776 982 1

*This book is dedicated to Madeleine*

*I count myself in nothing else so happy*
*As in a soul remembering my good friends*

Shakespeare

# Contents

# Acknowledgements

I wish to express my thanks to Sue and David Favell for the generous help they gave in the typing and preparation of my manuscript.

I am grateful to the editors of *Punch* magazine for giving me permission to use the illustrated poem 'Naval Wings', from their *Almanack for 1943*, as a frontispiece in my story.

I wish to thank the Ministry of Defence Publication Clearance Department for permission to include in my book the photographs obtained from official sources during my naval service.

## Naval Wings

IF you should stroll down Whitehall way
  Casting a curious eye
On this and that, your glance may fall
Upon a colonnaded wall,
And over it, set high
Above the massive central gate,
Two strange sea-monsters perched in state.

For nigh two hundred years they've kept
The Admiralty door
While Nelson, Collingwood and Keith
And old John Jervis passed beneath
And many a hundred more
Who faced the battle and the breeze
That we might ride and rule the seas.

Some long-dead sculptor's skilful hand
Fashioned those scaly steeds
With fish-like tails that they might wear
The suitably aquatic air
An Admiralty needs . . .
That's very clear, but can you tell
Just why he gave them wings as well?

I think perhaps that sculptor pierced
The veil of things to be
And seeing some far-distant day
Where new and mortal danger lay
For those who ride the sea,
He carved and set a warning there
That we must also rule the air!    J. S. H.

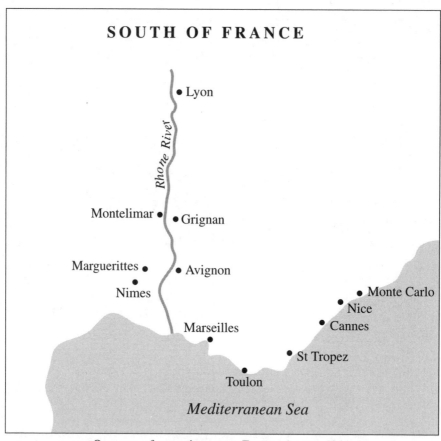

# SOUTH OF FRANCE

Rhone River

● Lyon

Montelimar ● ● Grignan

Marguerittes ● ● Avignon

● Nimes

● Monte Carlo
● Nice
Cannes

Marseilles

● St Tropez

Toulon

*Mediterranean Sea*

Our area of operations over France, August 1944

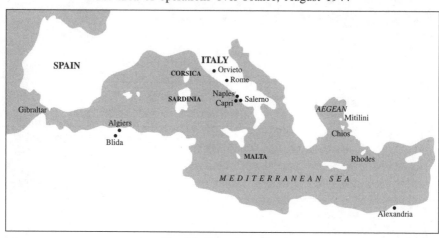

SPAIN

ITALY
CORSICA ● Orvieto
● Rome

SARDINIA    Naples ● ● Salerno
Capri ●

Gibraltar

*AEGEAN*
Mitilini

Algiers ●
● Blida

Chios

MALTA

Rhodes

*MEDITERRANEAN SEA*

Alexandria ●

The Mediterranean Sea

# *Prelude*

There were just four weeks before the trial was due to begin. The members of the court had been nominated. The charge document had been delivered and my signature had acknowledged its receipt. Any vague hopes for a change of heart by the authorities had now been dispelled.

The letter was written on a single sheet. It was short and succinct. With a sinking feeling I sat down to study it and, as my eyes scanned the text, the list of charges jumped at me from the page.

There was no way out now. The day on which the legal battle was to be fought had been designated. The moment of truth approached. My past reputation and my whole future were on the line. My fate was in the hands of others.

Where was my knowledge of lawyers and their procedures? Where was my skill at presenting a case? Nowhere! Who amongst my former colleagues would turn out to be my friends, and who my enemies? In large part I felt I knew the answers, but who might surprise me with their evidence in court?

Four weeks was more than long enough for me to ponder these questions, and to prepare myself for the ordeal ahead. With relief I found a friend to act in my defence. Together we made our preparations for the coming fight.

There was no way of avoiding the deep distress which was to be suffered by my wife and family, and by my parents when they received the news. How should I explain to them the circumstances of that fateful morning and, worse still, the humiliating charges laid against me? Would my explanations not seem unconvincing, and the complexities of the incident impossible to understand? But I had to let them know, and I must do so by letter to England,

1

across the ten thousand miles that separated them from me in distant Singapore. I knew what pain my letter would bring. Surely they would be consumed by questions to which they could obtain no answers, and tortured by doubts as to my integrity and honour. To reassure them from such a distance was impossible and I could hope only for their faith and trust.

The nature of the ordeal ahead was unfamiliar to me, and one far removed from any of the difficulties that I had faced in the past. In its own special way this predicament was as dangerous to me as any that I had known before and, in my mind, I knew that I must seek inspiration from the lessons I had learned during a long, eventful and often perilous career. Would the confidence and strength I needed be found in the fund of experiences gained in years gone by?

As those four weeks passed with agonising slowness, my waking thoughts and my dreaming hours dwelt upon the ups and downs of my past life, and upon the varied fortunes that had shaped me since the days of my childhood.

*Chapter 1*

# The Beginning (1923–41)

*The child is father to the man* – Wordsworth

On the western arm of Kootenay Lake lies the small settlement of Balfour. Here amongst the foothills of the Rocky Mountains of British Columbia I was born and spent my early childhood. If it were possible to pick the perfect place to start one's life, Balfour would be my choice. The lake, the mountains, the forests, the tumbling boulder-strewn creeks, the rainbow trout, the salmon, the orchards of apple and cherry; surely this was nature in perfection and, in those days, a land unspoiled by man. Our lives were shared with the bears, the lynx, the cougars, the gophers; wildlife in abundance.

In 1928 we moved to the more remote settlement of Riondel on the east side of the main lake. Here the Bluebell Mine produced lead, zinc and silver. My father, who had been seriously wounded during the second battle of Ypres in 1915, was Mine Accountant and, as Personnel Manager, was responsible for the engagement of the miners, for their accommodation, payment, living conditions and welfare. He ran the general store which catered for the varied requirements of the whole community.

Riondel was serviced by a fleet of 'sternwheelers', paddlesteamers which, since there were no roads, provided the sole means of transport between all the settlements round the lake. Nelson, the chief town of the Kootenay, was the focus for public offices, shopping and hospitals.

The skill of the sternwheeler crews was legendary. They coped with the routine transport needs of the area and with every emergency which arose, whatever the weather. Riondel had no doctor, and my

3

sister Ann was born aboard the SS *Kuskanook* whilst my mother was on her way to hospital in Kaslo. The Captain expressed the, perhaps forlorn, hope that she would be named after the vessel.

Each settlement made its own arrangements for agreeable living, and for its entertainment. As children, if we wanted toys we made them ourselves, and I believe we absorbed the independence of spirit which characterised the peoples of those communities in western Canada. Certainly my parents, like all their countrymen, never sought, nor expected, any welfare handouts from government. They worked ceaselessly all their lives to support themselves and their family, thereby receiving our devoted love and admiration.

Winters were cold, with frequent and heavy snowfalls. As children we learned early to get about on skis, a skill easily acquired when our centres of gravity were only a foot or so above ground level, and when falling over was painless. In spells of bad weather snowshoes were the customary footwear for short trips outside the home.

Inside the house a large furnace kept everything warm. It consumed great quantities of the logs which were stacked neatly under a sheltering roof at the side of the house. Sawing logs for firewood was a chore that occupied my father for endless hours during the weeks preceding the onset of winter. Inevitably my brother and I were dragooned unwillingly into assisting in any way we could with this task. The furnace, situated in the middle of the house, roared away merrily throughout the freezing months, keeping us in warm and snug comfort and, I suppose, assuring our survival.

During the warm and sunny months of summer the water became the chief focus of our childhood activities. The lake was usually calm but, in occasional storms, the surface could be severely disturbed and become a hazard to small boats. Driftwood was strewn all along the rocky edges of the lake, in the coves and upon the beaches. My elder brother, Barry, was an enthusiastic constructor of rafts. From the scatter of logs and planks he selected what he required to make a safe flat boat with a saw, a hammer and a few nails. As he paddled me round rocky headlands on clear water I was mesmerised by the submerged world which lay below.

The lake was home to the Kokanee salmon, a freshwater cousin to the Sockeye ocean species, the name meaning 'red fish' in the tongue of the Kutenai Indians. From a small boat, using rod and spinner or fly, my father could expect a catch of several salmon,

4

of weights up to 15 pounds, during a morning on the water. The fish made a steady and helpful contribution to our family diet and could be eaten fresh, or were smoked or bottled for storage. Other kinds of fish, chiefly rainbow trout, abounded in the creeks and rivers which flowed into the lake.

Our favourite beach and picnic spot lay not greatly distant from our home at Riondel. Called North Bay, it was accessible on foot; but this meant walking through a field in which the local farmer, Mr McGarvey, kept several large and fierce-looking bulls. I do not know that anyone was actually attacked, but the possibility of such an encounter was reason enough for us to make the journey to the beach by boat. Not only was this safer but it eased the problem of transporting food, drink and all the paraphernalia needed for an all-day beach party. With several families, numerous children and all their provisions aboard, these excursions to the beach by boat remain in my mind as memorable outings. Fires for cooking were easily assembled from driftwood, and splashing in the water and exploring the adjacent lakeside stimulated hearty appetites for the beach-grilled feast of chicken drumsticks, chops, corn cobs and potatoes prepared by the adults.

Were these idyllic days of childhood truly as gloriously happy as memory portrays? I believe they were and I have an abiding gratitude to my parents for giving me such a start in life.

In 1930, the Depression was so severe that the mine had to close and my parents decided to travel to the UK in hope of finding work. They bought the farmhouse Knockwood House, built in the late 15th century, at Nether Wallop in Hampshire. The Depression turned out to be just as severe in the UK as in Canada and the USA, and my father found it impossible to get a job – he was then 45 years old. It was a great struggle to find the means to educate the three of us kids.

My brother Barry went to Reigate Grammar School. My sister Ann went to the Royal Naval School at Twickenham and, later, at Haslemere. I went to Northwood Preparatory School at the age of seven and then to Christ's Hospital School at Horsham in Sussex. I did the first year in the Prep and then moved to Peele 'A' House, where I remained until 1941.

How fortunate I was to enjoy the great benefits offered by this school where the staff devoted their lives to 'The Royal, Religious and Ancient Foundation of Christ's Hospital'. The encouragement of effort was paramount in all fields, academic, sport and music, to name just three. Success was the goal in everything but inevitable failure was regarded as a spur to renewed effort and perseverance. Responsibility was fostered at each stage so that most activities in sport and domestic routine were organised by the boys themselves as they progressed towards seniority.

In music my violin lessons were later to prove an unexpected asset, as were the years spent learning French and German. I believe that the caring but demanding character of C.H. was of huge benefit to me in coping with the successes and setbacks that I encountered in later life. I feel the warmest affection and gratitude towards all those who made possible the seven years which I enjoyed at this greatest of all schools.

I believe that none amongst the countless thousands who have lived and toiled there can ever have disagreed with the school motto:

> *May those prosper who love it, and may*
> *God increase their number.*

During the school holidays in the latter part of August 1939 my sister Ann and I, with our parents, were spending a two-week break in a country cottage at Boldre, near Lymington, in the New Forest. To get there I had made the journey on my bicycle so that during the holiday I would be able to explore the surrounding areas of moorland and forest. We were blessed with fine warm weather but, on 3rd September, our stay at the delightful cottage was brought to a sudden and unscheduled end. On that morning, clustered round the radio in the sitting room, we listened as the Prime Minister, Neville Chamberlain, made his 11 o'clock broadcast. He told the nation that no undertaking by Hitler to cease his attack on Poland had been received and that, therefore, Britain was, from that moment, at war with Germany.

Although we had been well prepared for such an announcement, these words, when we heard them, came as a stunning shock. There had been descriptions of blitzkrieg tactics by the German forces in Poland and I think these led us to believe that we, too, would be subject instantly to such attacks from the Luftwaffe. My mother, who had lived through the First World War, and my father who

6

had been wounded at Ypres, had every reason to fear the worst and they decided that our holiday should be ended and that we should return home at once.

After packing up our belongings I prepared for the long bicycle-ride back to Knockwood. On departure my mother embraced me so tightly that I think she feared that I might well be strafed or bombed en route and that we might never meet again. In the event no sounds of war marred that sunny afternoon, though I kept a wary eye out for the enemy aircraft which I expected to appear overhead. We could not imagine then that there were to be seven months of 'phoney war' before the land and air battles in western Europe began in earnest.

Despite the excitement of the war we continued our schooling and our sports. On the cricket fields in the spring of 1940 we could hear the constant rumble of the guns, and feel the earth shudder, during the battles of the evacuation at Dunkirk. We spent many nights in the air-raid shelters, and from the top of Sharpenhurst Hill, where we did night duty armed with .303 rifles, we had a grandstand view of the London Blitz. The flash and flare of the burning city cast a trembling glow across our northern horizon. Searchlights waved and criss-crossed their slender fingers through the night sky. Spellbound, we watched and waited for the all-too-rare moment when the tiny image of a hated enemy glowed silver as, briefly, it was held transfixed in space. Our task was to catch any German airmen who parachuted down but we never had the thrill of doing so in my time, although a number of aircraft crashed in the neighbourhood of the school.

Our chapel accommodated the entire school of 850 boys, together with members of the teaching staff. A short 15-minute service was held each morning before the first session of classroom lessons. Attendance was compulsory, as it was for two full-length services every Sunday – matins and evensong. From time to time at the weekday service our Director of Music, Dr Lang, presided over a rehearsal for some forthcoming religious service or choral event. He had an authoritative manner which insisted upon the whole attention of every member of his large congregation. A perfectionist, he was satisfied with nothing less than full cooperation from the hundreds of ungifted voices, as well as from the enthusiastic and well-trained choir. He took the trouble to explain the reasons for the special demands which he made on us to achieve the result he

7

desired, and I believe that he was a much respected teacher who played an important part in our lives, especially when the school prepared for its taxing performance of a work such as Handel's *Messiah*. How often I recall the stirring sound of 850 boys in full voice. These chapel services made a lasting impression upon me, as I am sure they did on most boys at Christ's Hospital. All music, whether orchestral or band, was regarded as an important element in our education and every year the London Symphony Orchestra visited us to give a concert of classical music in 'Big School', our great assembly hall.

When reports came in of the death-in-action of former pupils, some of whom were recently our older schoolmates; when we saw evidence of the air battles in the skies above us and the wreckage of planes which crashed in our vicinity; when, each night, we watched the London Blitz in all its blazing fury we learned that, with so much violence and uncertainty in life, prayer was the essential source of inner strength if we were to face the unknown.

We played a lot of rugby in the winter, but no soccer. I was keen on the game, playing for some years in the three-quarter line and then, later, becoming a permanent full-back, perfectly placed to get the blame whenever the opposition scored a try! I never managed to get chosen to play for the school in the first 15, but I played for the second team when there was a flu epidemic and most of the regulars were in the sanatorium.

Shooting was my strongest line. We had a good indoor range at school and we travelled to the National Rifle Association base at Bisley in the summer months to shoot on the long ranges with .303 rifles. The Ashburton Shield was the great annual competition for all public schools. In 1939 I won a prize there – a Wedgwood and silver mug. I won the Duplessis Shield for indoor ranges with a then record score of 129 out of 130. This stood for many years but I have learnt that someone has since scored a 'possible'. How transitory is fame!

In the school holidays the unspoiled countryside round the Wallops offered limitless adventure. With my close friend Bill Cumberworth we fished the river brimming with trout, bagged rabbits for the pot and explored the country lanes and the rolling hills of Hampshire and Salisbury Plain on our bicycles.

Bill's parents lived by the river in a 'picture-book' cottage where there was always the warmest welcome. His father was a skilled fisherman who insisted that we learnt the rudiments of the sport before we were allowed to cast a dry fly on the water.

When I joined the Navy, Bill joined the Royal Air Force. On completion of his flying training he was posted to Coastal Command. On one fateful trip his four-engined ocean reconnaissance aircraft was lost without trace over the Atlantic and his name is inscribed amongst thousands of others on the tablets of the Runnymede memorial. I made a trip there in sadness to pay my respects to a boyhood pal who has no known grave. I must be glad that he, like me, enjoyed the freedom of the glorious English countryside in the years before the Second World War. The ploughman working his two shire-horse team exemplified the leisurely pace of life in those drowsy summer days of youth, when the chirruping song of soaring larks and the plaintive cries of lapwings filled our ears.


The war dominated all our lives and our thinking, and there was a powerful enthusiasm amongst most young people to get into the armed services and do their 'bit' for Britain, which was faring disastrously in every sphere. The airfield at Middle Wallop was built just before the war and the boundary fence was only a few hundred yards from Knockwood. During the summer school holidays of 1940 I watched the Spitfires and Hurricanes operating against the Luftwaffe in the great air battles which we could see above us. One day whilst helping a local farmer to get in the grain harvest we witnessed the airfield buildings being destroyed by a squadron of German dive-bombers.

I sat my School Certificate exam (equivalent to 'O' levels) in 1940 and managed to get the five credits required for matriculation. Unlike my sister, who went on to get her Higher Certificate, I recognised that I was an unlikely candidate for success in the higher exam and I concentrated on getting into the Royal Navy, which had long been my ambition (my maternal grandfather having reached the rank of Admiral). However, my experiences watching the air battles of 1940 led me to try to combine flying with a life at sea by applying for flying training as a pilot in the Fleet Air Arm.

In the early summer of 1941 I bade farewell to Christ's Hospital after seven eventful and largely happy years. Arriving home I filled in an application form to join the Royal Navy and, after being called to a selection centre in Bristol and having undergone my interviews and medical examinations, I was accepted for aircrew training by the Fleet Air Arm. This could not begin until I reached the age of 18, when I would start as a Naval Airman Second Class: the lowest of the low. The city of Bristol was a wasteland of almost total destruction after German bombing and the RN selection centre seemed to be one of the few buildings still intact.

A big demand for accommodation by military officers in the Salisbury area led my parents to rent Knockwood to an army family in order to raise some income. My father found and bought, for £350, a tiny two-bedroomed thatched cottage in the Somerset village of Barrington, near Ilminster. Named Pound Cottage, it was charming and cosy and, somehow, we all fitted in. At the Westland Aircraft Company factory at Yeovil, where Lysanders and twin-engined Whirlwinds were being built, I got a job in the Flight Shed. I cycled the 15 miles on hilly roads from Barrington, setting off each morning at 0545 to be at work by 0700. My darling mother got me out of bed every morning and gave me breakfast and a lunch pack before seeing me off on my journey. I finished work at 1700 and could expect to be home by 1815. My pay was $5\frac{1}{2}$ pence per hour, so for a day's work I received 4s 7d, equivalent today to 23p. For a week's work I earned £1 15p in today's money.

The highlight of my time at Westlands occurred when Harold Penrose, the Chief Test Pilot, offered to take me up for a flight in a Lysander. He gave me a short briefing on the use of my parachute and directed me to the rear cockpit. Finding that no seat had yet been fitted to it I was somewhat taken aback but Harold said, 'Never mind, just stand up.' Despite this rather disconcerting initiation to the world of flying the experience confirmed me in my enthusiasm to become a pilot. For the first time I had looked down on the sun-lit landscape of Somerset with its woods, fields and villages laid out below in immaculate and colourful pattern. This had been an inspiration to me and it made me more impatient than ever to get started on my aircrew training.

# Chapter 2

# Service Training (1942–3)

*'Begin at the beginning,' the King said gravely,*
*'and go on to the end, then stop.'* – Lewis Carroll.

With the winter approaching, I decided to try for a job which involved less travelling by bicycle. The headmaster of a prep school, which was evacuated from the south-east of England to Barrington Court, the estate of the Lyles of Tate and Lyle, took me on as a schoolmaster. I taught English, maths, history etc. to the younger boys, but was kept well away from classes preparing for the Common Entrance exams.

Whatever benefits of schooling I may have imparted to my pupils, my own education took a small step forward when, one balmy night in the rose garden, the young assistant matron permitted me a warm and encouraging kiss. Before this promising relationship could make any further progress, however, I received the long-awaited letter from the Admiralty instructing me to report to Lee-on-Solent on 12th January 1942 to commence my aircrew training.

We spent two weeks at Lee. We were kitted out as junior ratings in the Royal Navy and were given a fairly gentle introduction to what was to become a strict, demanding and very energetic regime of basic training when we moved to HMS *St Vincent* at Gosport. Here, for two months, we were shouted at and drilled, and, since no walking was permitted within the establishment at any time, we moved everywhere at the double. We did much classroom work on seamanship and aviation subjects, and learnt Morse-code communication by flash and buzzer, and semaphore. We scrubbed and polished, did firewatching duty on the roofs at night to cope with incendiary bombs and pulled whalers on freezing winter mornings in the icy waters of Portsmouth harbour.

Our main tormentor was Chief Petty Officer Wilmot, a Chief Gunner's Mate schooled in the traditions of strict and unswerving discipline instilled by the renowned Gunnery Establishment at Whale Island, near Portsmouth. He ran the whole of our routine during the months we spent at *St Vincent* and, except for the hours which we passed in classroom subjects such as navigation, seamanship and communications, he dominated our lives. Even by the standards of Whale Island he was an outstanding example of those martinets who were charged with the training of recruits. Like my fellow cadets, I could only wonder at his vocabulary, and at the flow and mode of expression which he used to instil instant obedience into us. A whole generation of RNVR aircrew cadets survived his demanding regime and I think all of us marvelled at his verbal dexterity and at his control of our lives, which was absolute. If he intended to strike fear and loathing into us, or if he ever tried to humiliate us, we soon came to realise that his manner was just a façade and any momentary hatred that may have been felt quickly turned to admiration and affection.

By whatever means Wilmot was found and chosen for this job, his selection was an inspired one. In the hearts of thousands of wartime aircrew this dedicated, brilliant and good man is held in grateful and fond remembrance.

By the end of the course we were fit and alert and, provided we passed our final exams, ready to progress to the next stage, the start of our flying training.

With the skies over Britain seething with warplanes both friendly and enemy, it was not practicable to carry out flying training within the UK. Great schemes for aircrew training had been set up in Canada and in Rhodesia, where cloudless skies allowed the training to be completed more rapidly than in Britain, even under peacetime conditions. The United States Navy, too, offered a full course to a limited number of British students.

With our final exams behind us we awaited eagerly the publication of lists allocating us to our country of training. When the list went up on the board I was thrilled to find my name in the group of about a dozen to go to the USA for fighter pilot training.

Before setting off we were given three days' leave. My parents came to Southsea and stayed at the prestigious Queens Hotel for a couple of nights. They remarked on how fit I looked and I assured them that it was all down to the attentions of Chief Petty Officer Wilmot. Dressed in my square rig Ordinary Seaman uniform, I took meals with my parents in the historic dining room of the hotel surrounded, at other tables, by very senior navy officers – Admirals, Captains and Commanders. After the three days' leave with my family to say hello and then farewell, we entrained for Greenock on the Clyde, staying at Heaton Park, Manchester, for two nights and a series of inoculations.

In the Clyde we embarked in the 11,000-ton ship *Banfora*. She was anchored in the midst of a huge number of vessels of all types which were to form our 5-knot Atlantic convoy. The voyage to Halifax, Nova Scotia, took 21 days and, with 2,558 persons encased within this small ship, the conditions on board were frightful. A hurricane off Iceland, when the whole convoy and escorts became separated and dispersed, made them worse. At this time our shipping losses in the north Atlantic were massive and unsustainable, and the bad weather probably ensured our safety, as U-boats could not operate effectively in such huge seas.

The north Atlantic crossing in this slow convoy seemed interminable. With limited opportunities for getting fresh air on deck, most of our time was spent within the cavernous holds of the ship, where we passed the hours sitting on benches at long wooden tables reading, writing letters or playing cards and board games. We took our meals in that same space and, at nightfall, prepared our hammocks for slinging on hooks fixed to beams across the deckhead. The hooks were spaced in such a way that when all our hammocks were slung they made a solid canopy of bulging canvas above the mess tables. For those not lucky enough to have been allocated a hammock, the mess tables became their bedsteads, whilst the remainder slept on the deck itself. How fortunate I was to be the lucky possessor of a hammock and fortunate, too, not to be incapacitated by seasickness, as many were. Those who slept upon the tables were, of course, vulnerable to those above them who were indisposed. Those on the deck itself, with two layers above them, were doubly exposed and suffered accordingly.

This was not a period in my life which I look back upon with any sense of pleasure, even though I slept in the top layer. When we sighted land our delight was unbounded and when at last we stepped ashore we neither wished, nor expected, ever to set eyes again on the SS *Banfora*, though we certainly felt thankful that our escorts had assured us a safe passage.

At Halifax we transferred to a train for Moncton, New Brunswick, where a transit camp held Fleet Air Arm and Royal Air Force students until they could be fed into their allotted flying training bases. We stayed at Moncton for about three weeks. After more than two years of blackout, the bright lights on the streets and in the shop windows turned the town into a thrilling wonderland for us. We feasted on chocolate, oranges, bananas, steaks and all the things we had only dreamed about for so long. This was an exciting time and we were allowed almost total freedom to enjoy the wonderful hospitality of the residents of this small town. I shall never forget their warmth and generosity.

The long-awaited day arrived when we made our journey from Moncton to the US Naval Air Station Grosse Ile, near Detroit, in Michigan. Here we began flight training in earnest. My instructor was Captain Robert Cameron of the US Marine Corps. Unlike a few of the instructors, who struck fear and even loathing into their pupils, Cameron was always patient and encouraging, though demanding of the highest standards. I was fortunate indeed. We were, of course, desperately keen to succeed and we were wholly absorbed in the challenge of learning to fly.

On 18th May Cameron took me up for the first time and I made my initial solo on 1st June. This memorable flight was made from the airfield owned by the Ford Motor Company at Dearborn, near Detroit. With a coloured streamer tied to a strut at my starboard wing tip, indicating to other aircraft that this was a pilot on first solo, I made my single circuit and landing, literally talking myself through the routine of every stage in the process. Cameron gave me the 'thumbs-up' when I taxied up to where he had been sitting on the grass, watching my every move. He clambered into his seat and with him I returned to Grosse Ile, a happy man. Though an early landmark in the training, this must be for all pilots one of the great moments of their lives.

Our days began at 0530 each morning and were split between ground school and flying. With the pressure of war we were given very little free time. We worked for seven days and then had one day off.

In the three months of US Navy primary training much of the syllabus was concentrated upon aerobatics. The proper recovery from a spin was emphasised early on as there was always the chance of getting into one by accident if a manoeuvre was poorly executed. We were trained in the standard aerobatic repertoire, including loops, wing-overs, immelmans (rolls off the top of a loop), barrel rolls and slow rolls. The biplanes on which we trained were robust enough to allow us to perform the snap-roll, an exhilarating manoeuvre not permitted, on grounds of strength, in any aircraft which I flew subsequently in my flying career.

Another feature of the training programme centred upon the precise control of the aircraft on its approach to a landing, and the accuracy needed to touch down exactly at a chosen spot. To this end a white painted circle with a diameter of, perhaps, 20 yards was described on an outlying field. From 500 feet, at a convenient distance downwind from the circle, the throttle was closed to idle power and the pilot was required to control his approach so as to make a three-point touch down within the circle. To achieve this end two methods were taught: firstly 'S-turns to circle shots'; secondly 'side-slips to circle shots'. In each case the strength of the wind governed the number of S-turns made or the severity of the side-slips which were required. We had to develop a fine judgement in these exercises and, with much practice, we became expert at our circle-shots. Unless wind conditions were exceptional all landings had to be three-pointers. This was insisted upon in all flying training schemes, but particularly in those for naval pilots, who would later be required to land on aircraft carriers.

Before our primary training was complete we made some simple cross-country navigational sorties, and were given an elementary introduction to flying in formation. On completion of each stage in the course we were required to undergo a check-flight with an instructor other than our own. These were much dreaded occasions, for failure at any stage meant either to be set back to repeat that part of the syllabus or, at worst, to be withdrawn from flying training.

After three months all my tests and exams were behind me and we bade farewell to Grosse Ile and made the two-day train journey to Pensacola in north Florida. All my flying until now had been in the beautiful, fully aerobatic biplane designated N3N3. Here at Elysson Field we flew monoplanes with retractable undercarriages for the first time. Throughout our training so far we had not had to concern ourselves with the position of the wheels, they had always been down. Now we had to raise them after take-off and lower them for landing. It was not unknown for a pilot to forget the latter and to make an excruciatingly expensive noise on touch-down, leaving the pupil not only extremely red-faced but highly unpopular with the engineers and the instructing staff.

At Pensacola we underwent two separate courses, one in formation flying and one in instrument flying. This last I found both difficult and unpleasant as hours were spent 'under the hood', experiencing the most extraordinary and worrying sensations, in near darkness.

Initially the pupil had to study the mechanism and working of each instrument on his blind flying panel, and to learn the way each one responded to the manoeuvres of the aircraft. Finally he had to master the technique of interpreting the messages the six instruments were sending him as they interacted. This required hours and hours of practice, many of which were spent on the ground in the Link Trainer, an early form of the very sophisticated simulators of more recent years.

The courses at Pensacola lasted for eight weeks and we then moved on to the US Naval Air Station Opa Locka, near Miami, for a lengthy and very intensive advanced course flying SNJ–3 (Harvard) aircraft. Now our training involved further exercises of the types we had made in earlier stages but at a more demanding level. We worked together with other students in making rendezvous, practised operating in various formations and learned the art of changing from one configuration to another without endangering the other aircraft. With plenty of time spent on aerobatics, including spins and the recovery from them, we prepared for the end-of-course demonstration of aerobatics which each student pilot had to perform before an audience of instructors watching from the ground.

As potential fighter pilots, we spent much time performing mock attacks on other aircraft and, at the same time, studying the optimum techniques for avoiding our own destruction by enemy fighters. Numerous sorties were made over the sea, firing our guns at sleeve targets towed by one of our colleagues.

Cross-country navigation exercises by day and, later, by night were made over southern Florida. These were relatively simple by day as prominent landmarks abounded and, if they were roads or railways, they tended to run in straight lines for miles and miles on end. By night, with no blackout, the towns and the roads were easily identified. With the stars above, and the carpet of lights below, it was a magical world. How different this was to be when we returned to the United Kingdom, where total blackout prevailed and where, more often than not, the night sky was obscured by cloud.

From time to time we were again put 'under the hood' by our instructor in continuation of our training in flying blind on instruments. To improve our skill in this aspect of aviation was an essential part of the course. On the ground, periods in the Link Trainer were recurring items in our curriculum.

Ground school continued to be a part of each day's work. We studied the design of engines and the proper handling and control of them by the pilot. The vital importance of this was stressed again and again. We learned the techniques of flying for maximum range, and for maximum endurance. Paper exercises in air navigation, and in the use of maps for cross-country flights, were a valued part of the syllabus, as was an extensive series of classes on meteorology. All in all we were kept hard at it each day from an early morning start. Once in bed at night sleep came in an instant and, if we dreamed, it was of the 24-hour break which we were permitted every eighth day.

On completion of this advanced stage of the course we were awarded our United States Navy 'wings' – a proud moment in our lives. This achievement was marked by my promotion from Leading Naval Airman to Midshipman RNVR, and by the consequent right to enjoy the amenities of the Officers' Club – chiefly the bar.

Now came the final stage of the US Navy training, known as a 'pre-operational'. For the first time we were to fly single-seat fighter aircraft and consequently no dual instruction beforehand could be given. My first flight in the Brewster 'Buffalo', with an engine producing two or three times the power of anything I had known before, was an experience not to be forgotten. Getting it into the air and landing it again in one piece was something of a near miracle. It was more a case of the aircraft flying me than of me flying it.

The Florida Everglades or the Atlantic Ocean formed the backdrop to most of our flying from Opa Locka, with the Tamiami Trail, a long straight highway running north–south, our most reliable aid to navigation. The weather during our four-month training period was invariably fine, interrupted by regular, almost daily, thunder-storms. The white cumulus clouds which often filled the skies formed an irresistible aerial playground through and around which we zoomed and flashed, climbed, rolled and dived in exhilaration. In those days flying was for the few only and we knew we were privileged to revel in this magical world, unknown to others.

The training programme was, however, intensive and we had little free time. Every eighth day was a holiday when we made the most of our opportunity to enjoy the delights of Miami. This was centred largely upon Walgreens Drug Store, where we tested the multitude of exciting concoctions – milkshakes, ice creams, sodas, sundaes, meringue pies, all delights which we knew we would miss when we returned to war-torn Europe. At Miami Beach we were made particularly welcome by the Lord Tarleton, one of many ultra-modern hotels stretching the length of the beach. The swimming pool and the sea became the focus of our lives before the moment arrived when we must return to base for another seven days' hard work.

To hire a car for 24 hours was simplicity itself, but a driving licence had to be presented to the rental compamy. When I applied for a licence from the appropriate authority I was asked to give my name, age, address and details of my occupation. When I explained that I was undergoing the advanced stage of flying training at Opa Locka the official said 'OK – if you can fly an airplane you can drive a car – here's your licence.'

Even on our meagre wages the hire of a car was an affordable luxury, expeically with the low cost of petrol. Once we were on the road, the delights of southern Florida opened up before us as we explored the palm-strewn coastal areas, delighting in the warm air scented by a land everywhere carpeted with brightly coloured tropic flowers and shrubs. Orange trees and grapefruit bushes abounded and, in our time, were laden with fruit. The ripe grapefruit picked straight from the tree were sun-warmed, pink, sweet and delectable. Americans, with their legendary friendliness, were ever interested to talk to us about Britain and the war in Europe, especially the German bombing of our cities. With unfailing hospitality they took us into their homes, plied us with food and drink and introduced

18

us to their friends. All too soon our short break was over and the race began to get back to base before our allotted time was up, and we faced another seven days' work.

All true fighter planes in those days were single-seaters. The pilot, being on his own without help from another crew member, was driver, navigator, tactician, engineer, radio operator, gunner and bomb-aimer. His training therefore had to equip him to manage all these functions unaided. It was many years before I was to experience the luxury of flying with a crew of specialists who could be called upon for expert advice.

My log book showed 289 flying hours when my US training came to an end and we received our coveted certificates and our 'wings' from the Base Commander. With sadness we bade farewell to Miami and entrained for the two-day rail journey to New York, where we spent a few days over Christmas staying at the Barbizon Plaza Hotel. Parties and generous hospitality were offered widely by friendly Americans. Whilst we were in New York the British war film *In Which We Serve* was being screened in movie houses throughout the city. Most of the population seemed to have watched the film and any men dressed in the uniform of the Royal Navy, as we were, could be assured of being hailed in the street, 'Hi, Bud! Let me buy you a drink. There's a bar right across the road. Have you been sunk yet...?' and so on, and on. After our long months of training these were wondrous days to savour. Even though we realised that our popularity was undeserved, and that we had yet to earn any right to be acclaimed, we lapped up all the open-hearted bonhomie and took it in our stride. I think every one of us made it to the top of the Empire State Building and I supped at the 21 Club but, all too soon, it was down to the docks to embark in our troopship for return to the UK.

In the berth next to the burnt-out hull of the mighty French liner *Normandie* we climbed the gangplank of the troopship which was to carry us home. She turned out to be the *Banfora*, the same vessel in which we had crossed the Atlantic almost a year before. We could hardly believe our misfortune and this unpleasant surprise filled us with gloom. It was hard to accept that, with so many hundreds of ships on the transatlantic run, we could twice be so afflicted. As things turned out, however, our accommodation was hugely better. As officers, we were given cabins with proper berths. Crowded, yes, but clean and with the use of adequate public rooms.

Many of our fellow passengers were American army officers, together with a contingent of US Red Cross nurses. In this congenial company we made no complaints on our voyage home. Not so for some of the American officers, who had a hard time dealing with the near-mutinous discontent of the hundreds of their soldiers who were enduring the same foul conditions in the holds that we had known on our voyage out to Canada the previous year. However, the slow convoy across the wintry Atlantic ended without mishap and we arrived off Gourock in the Clyde estuary in late January 1943.

Before completing our flying training we were given a three-week course at the Royal Naval College, Greenwich. In these impressive surroundings we attended lectures on a range of cultural subjects – naval history, service customs and traditions and the relationships between officers and ratings. We took our meals in the magnificent Painted Hall of the college. Good behaviour and manners in the mess were emphasised as a means towards ensuring a happy atmosphere in the wardroom, where we could expect to spend long months at sea in a confined space.

During a psychology session our lecturer gave a piece of advice which I have always remembered – in fact about the only item in the course which has stuck in my mind. He counselled us never to use the expression 'I must not forget to ... but always say 'I must remember to...' By using the former the sense of forgetfulness is implanted in the subconscious and forget is what one will do. By using the latter the reverse will be the case. I have found this advice to be sound and I have thus remembered to mention it.

After a few days' leave we began a series of courses designed to fit us for operating and fighting in European weather conditions, and in British fighter aircraft from both airfields and aircraft carriers.

At Hinstock, near Shrewsbury, we spent hours flying on instruments. During training in the USA we rarely encountered bad weather, but now we were faced with cloudy conditions on most days and we quickly realised that this constituted a serious challenge to our survival.

At RNAS Yeovilton we converted to Hurricanes. By day we coped with the weather and by night we took off from a runway delineated by glim lamps and flew over a blacked-out countryside in pitch darkness. What a contrast from our night flying in the

USA, where the cities and roads were brightly lit and navigation was simple. How I ever took off in my Hurricane, flew a short cross-country, found my way back to Yeovilton and landed safely on a dark night has been a source of astonishment to me ever since. The glim lamps edging the runway were visible only when we reached final approach and the light they gave was minimal.

At RAF Warmwell in Dorset we flew our Hurricanes over the Channel to fire our guns at sleeve targets pulled by towing aircraft.

Back at Yeovilton, we spent hours practising aerodrome dummy deck landings (ADDLs) in preparation for our first visit to an aircraft carrier. The moment of truth for all naval aviators was looming closer every day and we approached it with not a little dread. The most precise control of the aircraft in speed, rate of descent and pattern of approach was required to make a safe arrival on deck. Few other manoeuvres called for such intense concentration. Most of our carriers were small, and more recent developments such as the angled deck, the mirror landing aid and vertical take-off and landing did not exist. When the day came I made my four Hurricane deck landings on the small aircraft carrier HMS *Vindex* in the Clyde estuary. This earned me my qualification as a Royal Naval Aviator. I received it with pride and considerable relief.

Before leaving Yeovilton I flew the Spitfire for the first time. As I entered this in my log book I enjoyed the indescribable feeling of elation that all pilots experienced who were privileged to fly this beautiful and already famous aircraft.

My parents' home at Barrington was only a few minutes' flying time from Yeovilton. The temptation to give them a 'beat-up' had to be resisted and, except on a very few occasions when the desire became irresistible, it was. This type of enterprise was seriously frowned upon by those who governed our lives, and who had the power to issue us with a Red Endorsement, or worse.


My departure from Yeovilton in early 1943 marked the end of my formal flying training and, with 341 hours in my log book, I was appointed to RNAS Donibristle in Fife to join the ferry pool based there. This air station received new aircraft from the factories, prepared them for squadron service, and despatched them to bases all over the United Kingdom. In addition the engineering department repaired damaged aircraft and performed major overhauls on others.

21

These too had to be flown away to their designated squadrons. My job, with the other pilots of the pool, was to fly them there. This involved delivering planes to bases all over the country from the Orkneys in the north to airfields on the south coast of England. We flew many different types of aircraft and weather conditions were often extremely difficult. No effective navigational aids existed in those days and I realised very soon that the lengthy training I had received was just a minimal basis on which to develop my skills.

On one occasion, delivering a Spitfire to RNAS Machrihanish, the into-wind runway was closed. A gale was blowing and the direction of the wind was at a right-angle to the only runway available. With its narrow undercarriage, the Spitfire was susceptible to such conditions. Despite this I kept it on the runway for most of the landing run but, eventually, I could not prevent one wheel slipping off the edge. It ran into a patch of soft gravel and this caused the nose to drop. It dug in and the aircraft overturned, so that the cockpit, and my head inside it, came into violent contact with the ground. I was unconscious for a few minutes while the rescue services released me. I felt fine for a while afterwards but later I developed a serious headache and was flown back to Donibristle. The concussion I suffered put me into Dunfermline hospital for a few days.

A frequent and popular destination was the air station at Hatston in the Orkneys. Here it was standard practice to pick up a couple of dozen freshly laid eggs from local farmers and bring them back to the mainland, where eggs were rationed to one per week (or was it one per month?) Whichever it was, these treasures were regarded as gold dust in shells. If butter and dried fruit were obtainable they could even be used to bake a rich fruit cake, an almost forgotten luxury which most people thought of only in their dreams.

At Christchurch on the south coast of Hampshire the Airspeed Aviation Company was contracted to modify early model Seafires by replacing their Rolls Royce Merlin engines with advanced and more powerful Merlins. These gave the aircraft a greatly enhanced performance, especially at flight levels below 20,000 feet. The Airspeed factory had its own small grass airfield, so small in fact that the grass was deliberately allowed to grow to waist height. This had the desired effect of acting as a brake on the aircraft during its landing run, so preventing an overshoot into the far boundary of the field. Even for a naval pilot, schooled in the art of landing aboard a small aircraft carrier, the approach and landing at Christchurch presented quite a challenge.

One day a close friend and colleague landed there but, despite the long grass, he realised after touching down that he was going to overshoot the field. He therefore opened up to go round again for another try but, though his Seafire lifted off the ground, it did not gain enough height to avoid a house on the boundary. Fortunately nobody was home at the time, but the house and the aircraft were wrecked and the pilot was seriously injured. He had made a Hatston 'egg-run' shortly before his Christchurch delivery flight and two dozen eggs were stowed in his Seafire. They were destined as a present for his mother, who lived in the south. When the wreckage of his aircraft was extricated from what remained of the house, a carefully insulated box was discovered within a wing panel stowage. It was found to contain 24 unbroken fresh eggs. It is sad to relate that they never reached his mother.

In hospital my friend made a lengthy but successful recovery from his head injuries. He flew on operations for the next three years of war, earning the award of two Distinguished Service Crosses and later, in peacetime, an Air Force Cross.

# Chapter 3

# In the First Line (1943–4)

*We watched the ocean and the sky together*
*Under the roof of blue Italian weather* – Shelley

By midsummer I was appointed to a first-line fighter squadron, No. 879. Before joining them I was to attach myself to No. 809 Squadron at RAF Andover to undergo an army cooperation course. This covered aerial photography, tactical reconnaissance, artillery and gunnery support. Many sorties involved a low-level transit to a distant target which was to be photographed by oblique or vertical cameras. 'Low level' meant exactly that – as low as it was possible to fly and still avoid hitting trees, power lines or church steeples. Only in wartime was such activity permitted, though these flights were exhilarating in the extreme. Navigation was entirely by map reading which, at a high speed and at such a low level, demanded a great deal of practice. To make these long and exciting overland flights at 'nought-feet', and know that we would not be prosecuted for it, gave us delight and a special satisfaction.

Some exercises were made at a higher altitude, perhaps when a line of territory was to be photographed from directly above. This required a series of photographs to be taken with each picture overlapping the previous one. This was known as the 'vertical line overlap'. These pictures would then be examined on the ground by an interpreter using a stereoscope which gave a 3-D effect, and a remarkably well defined image of objects in the picture.

In cooperation with the army gunners at Lark Hill we practised the art of spotting for the artillery. The exercise was a demanding one for the pilot as he had to manoeuvre his aircraft so as to ensure that he was in a position to see the explosion of a shell when it struck the ground. Having observed the fall of shot, he then had to give instructions to the gunners to adjust their aim so that the next shot landed nearer the target. This procedure continued until the desired result was achieved. To see for ourselves how the gunners did their side of the job at ground level, we spent the occasional day with them on the artillery ranges at Lark Hill. Not only was this a useful exercise in cooperation but at lunchtime in their splendid mess we enjoyed a meal superior in quality and choice to anything we had known at a Royal Navy or Royal Air Force mess anywhere in the country. Despite wartime rationing, the gunners obviously knew something nobody else did.

It was gratifying that the army gunners were willing to accept instructions from a navy pilot but, when we did similar work with the Royal Navy, known as 'bombardment spotting', it was unsurprising that they would not accept orders from an aviator. They required him to inform them of the position of the fall of shot, then they would decide what correction of aim was required. Each of the two systems needed its own procedure and, being very different, they took a lot of practice if perfection was to be achieved.


On completion of this course I made my way to RNAS Machrihanish at the Mull of Kintyre to join No. 879 Squadron, flying Seafires. After only a couple of weeks getting to know my new colleagues we embarked in our carrier, HMS *Attacker*, and sailed as escort to a convoy for the Mediterranean. Flying from North Front airfield at Gibraltar we did hours of fighter patrols of the area, together with air firing practices.

One night in my cabin I was woken from a deep sleep to find my brother Barry standing by my bunk. I had not seen him since 1937, six years earlier when he had left for a job in India. I had no knowledge that he was in Gibraltar. His ship, HMIS *Jumna*, had been in the Mediterranean to support the allied landings in Sicily. Following that they made a short visit to Gibraltar. Barry had been ashore for an evening and, at around midnight, by chance one of *Attacker*'s boats came along and offered to drop him off at his ship. He said he thought his brother might be aboard *Attacker* – he had had no idea before this that we were amongst the many warships in the harbour. Thus it was that we had a remarkable, but very brief, reunion. I went with him to *Jumna*, where, over many glasses, we passed the rest of the night. *Jumna* sailed early in the morning and I was not to see Barry again until the war had ended.

In the first half of September 1943 we supported the amphibious landings by allied forces at Salerno by patrolling the skies over the Capri and Naples areas. With the fall of Sicily, and with our forces once again on the mainland of Europe, the plan was to land British and American troops behind the German lines in Italy. Because of poor security the enemy were aware that a landing was imminent, and that it was to be in the Naples area. As a result the assaulting troops in the Bay of Salerno met very strong resistance and, at one stage, after three days of desperate fighting, the allied command did fear that a withdrawal might be forced upon them. Gradually, however, the armies consolidated their positions and, eventually, they began to break out from their bridgehead.

Five small British aircraft carriers, *Attacker*, *Hunter*, *Stalker*, *Battler* and *Unicorn*, each with two squadrons of Seafires embarked, were stationed offshore to give air cover support for the invasion force. Two large Fleet carriers, *Formidable* and *Illustrious*, together with the four battleships *Rodney*, *Nelson*, *Warspite* and *Valiant*, were charged with providing air cover for the fleet of small assault carriers, and to counter any possible interference by enemy warships. From the five assault carriers a patrol of 16 fighters was maintained continuously on station over the invasion area from dawn to dusk each day. We patrolled at 16,000 feet over the Naples–Salerno region, looking down on the exquisite island of Capri lying beneath us in an unruffled blue sea. It was obvious, even from a great height, why this isle was chosen as the perfect place to call home by Gracie Fields and numerous other wealthy celebrities. Axel Munthe's book *The Story of San Michele* so well describes the compelling attraction of this sun-kissed isle.

Although the Germans put up the fiercest resistance to our armies on the ground, they did not offer any large-scale opposition to our fighter patrols. When they did attack us, the Luftwaffe did so with Messerschmitt 109s or Focke Wulf 190s in flights of four aircraft. From way above us they made tip-and-run attacks by descending upon us at a great rate, making one quick-firing run at a target, then instantly continuing their high-speed dive down to sea level and away to safety. On two occasions my formation was attacked in this way and, despite the huge speed differential achieved by these fast-diving attacks, my section leader, George Ogilvy, with speedy reaction and a bit of luck, managed to get behind one Me 109 and destroy it whilst it was making its high-speed escape. On another occasion an American Air Force P38 Lightning twin-boom fighter, one of four flying close on my port side, was attacked by FW 190s. It was hit by a stream of fire and exploded into fragments. I can still see the picture in my mind's eye.

When these attacks occurred it was every pilot's wish to get on the tail of an enemy, but the Germans had such a speed advantage, having dived on us from a great height, that to do so was a pretty forlorn hope. As part of a group of 20 aircraft, 16 Seafires and 4 Lightnings in open formation, the sky was pleasantly filled with friendly fighters. Following an enemy attack, with everyone seeking a target, suddenly the sky seemed empty. One minute we were surrounded by friends on all sides; seconds later there was not an aircraft to be seen anywhere. Then, isolated and alone, we felt highly vulnerable until, somehow, we got together again to resume our patrol. Everyone lived through this same amazing experience.

Throughout the entire assault stage of the Salerno landings the weather was fine, though visibility over a 'glassy' sea was poor, with a thick haze obscuring the ships and causing a problem of sighting the carriers when returning from a sortie, usually low on fuel. More serious than this, though, was the lack of wind. A complete calm prevailed throughout the five days of our operations. This compounded the difficulty of landing the Seafire on the deck of an escort carrier. These ships had a maximum speed of only 17 knots and often, with a dirty bottom after weeks at sea, they struggled to make 16 knots. The total length of the flight deck was a mere 420 feet, of which only the first 150 feet was available for engaging an arrester wire on touch-down. In ideal conditions the Seafire, with its long, wide nose obscuring the pilot's view ahead, was never an easy aircraft to deck-land but, under the circumstances at Salerno, it was extremely hazardous. Many aircraft were lost or damaged on their return to the deck.

We operated for a while longer in the Mediterranean and then returned to RAF Andover for further training in army support. Most of the pilots flew south from the ship but I was detailed by the CO as Officer-in-Charge of the draft of squadron ratings to make the journey by train, setting off from Gourock with about 100 men. We had to change at Glasgow, catch the night train to Euston, cross London to Waterloo and thence to Andover. The trains, of course, stopped at numerous stations on our long journey and I was very concerned on reaching our destination to find that I had far fewer men than I had started with at Gourock. I feared the wrath of the squadron Commanding Officer when I was summoned to his office. With trepidation I gave him my account of the journey. I was astounded when he congratulated me for losing only 12 sailors. Oh, happy day!

At Andover we concentrated particularly on tactical and photographic reconnaissance. Our specially adapted Seafires, Mark L-111, carried both oblique and vertical cameras. We spent a period at the Royal Naval Air Station Burscough, near Liverpool, updating our training in fighter tactics, and in dive-bombing and other ground attack techniques.

My first Squadron Commanding Officer was Lieutenant Commander Dick Gross, RNVR. He was only 23 years old but, since most of my fellow pilots were only 18 or 19 years of age, we regarded him as a vastly experienced old man. This situation was commonplace in those days because so many of the pilots who were flying at the start of the war had by then been killed.

The squadron was divided into three flights of four. Each flight was subdivided into two sections. For the greater part of my time in 879 Squadron I flew as No. 2 to George Ogilvy, the senior flight leader. Much of our work was on photographic and tactical reconnaissance, and we developed a close bond of trust and understanding. This was of crucial importance because radio silence was usually the order of the day.

George was a very able fighter pilot. He was, and has remained, a firm friend. Before taking up flying he had been at sea in two different ships, each of which had been sunk under him, one in the North Sea, one in the Channel off Calais. It was a comfort to be associated with such a well-established survivor. As an aerial reconnaissance pilot in tactical support of the army, he had a remarkable knack of seeking out the enemy, despite their best efforts at camouflage. His uncanny skill in this aspect of our flying was amazing to me. I never managed to match his expertise.

29

In the autumn of 1943 the command of the squadron was taken over by Lieutenant Commander David Carlisle. A South African from Durban, he very quickly earned our respect and trust and I knew that I was most fortunate to be led by such an agreeable and competent man. To this day we hold him in great affection.

The two Seafire squadrons in *Attacker*, No. 879 and No. 886, then amalgamated into one squadron of 24 aircraft. Each of the other three carriers with which we operated, *Hunter*, *Stalker* and *Battler*, amalgamated their squadrons in the same way and the whole became No. 4 Wing, with 96 Seafires and the same number of pilots. Lieutenant Commander George Baldwin, formerly CO of one of the squadrons, became Wing Leader. George was a natural leader, much admired by all of us, and a highly experienced and skilled aviator. We could not have been better led.

Many hours were spent developing the optimum tactics for carrying out fighter patrols. The easiest way for a leader to maintain control of the other aircraft in a squadron is to keep them in close formation. In this arrangement, however, each pilot must give his whole concentration to holding his position within the group. It is impossible for him to give attention to what is going on in the wider airspace. In the earlier stages of the war it had become obvious that single-seat aircraft, if they were in close formation, were vulnerable in the extreme to enemy fighter attacks. They could so easily come unobserved, out of the blue. By the time I came on the scene, special tactics had been developed to ensure that each pilot in a group was able to keep watch on the other members whilst the leader was still able to maintain control.

To ensure that each pilot watched over his colleagues, the ideal arrangement was to hold the aircraft in an open, line-abreast formation, with the planes about 30 or so yards apart. The pilots were then able to keep a good 'all-round' look-out. This disposition was fine while the leader continued to fly on in a straight line, but when he wished to change direction special manoeuvres were required of his wing-men. They must pass across and under him so that, on completion of his turn, the aircraft were again in line abreast. These evolutions were known as 'cross-over-turns'. Because radio silence prevailed the leader gave indication of his intention to change direction in, say, five seconds by making predetermined wing-rocking movements. The extent of the direction change determined the way in which the cross-overs were made and much

30

practice was needed to achieve perfect results. These manoeuvres, when properly executed, meant that no changes of engine power needed to be made by the wing-men on either side of the leader. In this manner the high fuel consumption which would result from power changes was avoided. We became expert at this technique; the manoeuvres, when well executed, gave great satisfaction, and the object of guarding our mates from surprise attack was achieved.

After spells at sea it was usually to the Clyde, Belfast or, occasionally, to Liverpool that we returned so that our ship could be docked for a short refit. As a squadron, we would fly off to a convenient airfield, where we would continue our training and, if we were lucky, enjoy a week or ten days' leave.

For me the passage home to my parents at Barrington in Somerset meant a long train journey. The rhythmic *dee-dum, dee-dum* beat of the carriage wheels as they crossed the joints in the rails played a joyous song in my ears. Every beat brought home nearer by a few yards.

Once back in the quiet and delightful West Country village, family life was resumed, old friends were visited, and a leisurely beer was enjoyed at the Royal Oak, our local pub. After much tinkering even my ancient motor bike was persuaded to burst into life. Renewed acquaintance was made with my favourite horse, which a friendly farmer had always allowed me to ride. Sauntering through the leafy lanes and bridleways of Somerset was relaxation at its best, and a perfect antidote to the rigours of wartime flying, so long as I resisted the temptation to try any jumps at fences or hedges. I had long since learned the hard way that anything higher than beginners' jumps required much more skill than I possessed. I had sometimes surmounted hedges but, more often than not, it was when the horse refused and I made it over on my own. On other occasions, when the horse took the jump I had been left behind.

All too soon my few days' leave were over, family farewells were made and the long unwelcome rail journey back to the ship or squadron began. Now the wheels of the train sang a different song. Each gloomy beat on the rails measured more yards from home and more yards nearer to the unknown prospect ahead. The rhythmic sounds of travel by train on bolted rails have, for all my life since then, reminded me of the feelings engendered in those wartime days.

By January 1944 we were again aboard HMS *Attacker*, flying from the carrier in waters off the west coast of Scotland, and sometimes operating from RAF Long Kesh (later home to the Maze prison!). The air station at Long Kesh was within easy travelling distance of Belfast, either by road or by train. In a small town on the road route, one enterprising member of our squadron had reached an agreement with the proprietor of a cosy eating place to provide us with a meal of steak and eggs, a special treat unknown to us on the mainland in those days of rationing. The steak was tender, the eggs were fresh and, when opportunities arose we repeated our visits to this friendly eatery. Following a pint or two of Worthington No. 3, or draught Guinness, or sometimes the two mixed together in equal quantities, these exceptional evening meals became landmarks in our lives.

In Belfast we were drawn to the joint services' officers' club. A large multi-storeyed building, it sported a bar on each of three floors and dancing on another. The club was invariably crowded with navy, army and air force officers from many nations. All branches of the American forces were much in evidence. They were massing in Northern Ireland in the same way as they were in all other parts of the United Kingdom prior to the launching of the allied assaults on the European mainland. Officers from France, Poland, Norway and the Dominions mixed with those from Britain and Ireland in this well-known and much favoured night spot. The last train from Belfast resounded with song and laughter, whilst the Wing Commander from the air station rode the footplate, claiming that he would ensure our safe return to base. I remember the Belfast Officers' Club as a fount of multi-national good will. It retains a place in my recollections of happy, though fleeting, times in those wartime days.

One day we sailed north from Scapa Flow in support of a Russian convoy but, after only a couple of days, we were ordered to turn round and head again for the Mediterranean, escorting a convoy en route. Back at Gibraltar, we operated from North Front as German aircraft were expected to attack the Rock. One night, when we were all asleep on board, they did, and *Attacker*, lying alongside the detached mole, an isolated berthing quay at the seaward boundary of the harbour, bore the brunt of an aerial torpedo assault. There

32

was an almighty *crump*. The ship surged and swayed, all the lights went out and my bunk reading lamp burst into fragments on the bed. We made our way to the upper decks to find that the ship had been mostly protected by the mole itself and that the damage was not serious, although the shape of the hull was afterwards not quite what it had been before the attack.

The short spells that we spent at Gibraltar were always popular. If our visit to the Rock was to be more than just a fleeting one, we flew off before the ship arrived and based our squadron at North Front airfield. From there we resumed our training in fighter patrols and tactics. In order to keep clear of Spanish airspace over Algeciras Bay the landing circuit was right-handed, or clockwise, when an easterly wind prevailed. A customary left-handed circuit was made when the wind was westerly but, in each case, the circuit encompassed the entire Gibraltar peninsula. This complicated the process of making the practice, or 'dummy', deck landings that were desirable before re-embarking in our carrier. Flying from a shore base instead of from the deck made a pleasant and stress-free change in our lives; taking off from a long runway and landing on it after each flight greatly relieved the tension of such operations aboard a carrier.

Beyond the pleasures and simplicities of flying from an airfield, Gibraltar offered many attractions. A sandy bay on the eastern shore of the colony could be reached on foot via a long and dripping tunnel which ran through the base of the Rock, starting at the dockyard on the western side where our ship was docked. At the bay, usually bathed in warm sunshine, we could enjoy good swimming and, if we were lucky, the company of Wrens, of which there were many employed in the various naval and allied staffs. In the evenings the Rock Hotel, overlooking the harbour, was a crowded rendezvous, whilst in the town the Gloucester Hotel bar was a favourite of our squadron. The fabled open-air night spots in Main Street with their dancing girls were a noisy delight, heavily patronised by sailors of many nations. Even in wartime the shops were stocked with goods unobtainable in Britain. All these made a stay at the intriguing and unique port of Gibraltar something to relish and, for me, the days we spent there are happy memories.

Early June found us based at RAF Blida in the desert south of Algiers. With our flying clothing soaked in sweat, we stood by our aircraft in sweltering heat to respond instantly to any scramble call when enemy aircraft were detected approaching the African coast. Any routine flying required we did at dawn in the cool of the morning. The airfield lay on the plain below the Atlas Mountains. As soon as the sun came up it became exceedingly hot and, over the bare mountains, the atmosphere was disturbed by violently rising and falling air currents. Although our aircraft were robust enough to survive the shocks of this turbulence, the 'bumps' we experienced here when flying at low level were the most severe I encountered in my flying career. They tested the limits of our own physical endurance so that unless we were scrambled, we avoided flying in the heat of the day. It was better to get up at five in the morning, have a cup of tea, and make any necessary flights before breakfast.

On occasion we were able to gain a brief respite by taking our jeep, driven by George, up into the foothills of the mountains to the charming resort of Chrea, a settlement much favoured, in peace time, by the French colonists of Algeria. Here, several thousands of feet above the plain, we enjoyed a breath of cool fresh air as we explored the village, or sat in the shade of a cedar tree to admire the view over a wide expanse of burning desert to the south. If any pilots of the squadron were flying that afternoon we could expect them to pay us a fleeting visit and make a high-speed pass to spoil the peace and tranquillity of this delightful refuge.

When *Attacker* was anchored in Algiers harbour we could perhaps spend a night on board, renew acquaintance with our non-flying shipmates, and make a sortie into Algiers to visit the fleshpots of the city, usually the bar of the Hotel Alletti, much frequented by officers of assorted nationalities, particularly Americans.


In July I was seconded to No. 2 Squadron, flying Spitfires as part of No. 7 Wing, South African Air Force, based at a forward grass airfield near Orvieto in Italy. The field was situated on high ground overlooking the city, with its tall cathedral spire reaching up from the valley below. I know now that Orvieto is noted for its fine white wine, but in all the time we were there I do not believe that we tasted a drop, or that we ventured even once into the town. At the end of each day we downed a glass of beer and ate our dinner in the big mess marquee. Before turning in we took a stroll around the edges of the field, listening to the incessant song of the crickets and watching the glimmering fireflies as they darted hither and thither in the soft evening air, flashing their little sparks of light.

Our task was support for the army whose front line at that time ran through Arezzo. We flew in flights of four and on each trip we were briefed to dive-bomb a specific target with our one 500-pounder. After delivering this we became 'freelance' for the remainder of our sortie, which generally lasted about 1 hour 20 minutes. We ranged freely over enemy territory and attacked any road and rail targets we could find, using cannon and machine guns. The countryside below us looked glorious in the summer sunshine and was some of the most beautiful I have ever seen, but anti-aircraft fire tracked us everywhere and at specific targets it was intense. From their 20mm and 40mm cannon the enemy put up what appeared to be an impenetrable cloud of anti-aircraft fire as we made our dives. The tracer shells ascended in a continuous chain of orange and yellow balls of fire. These seemed to hang in space until, suddenly, they were flashing in a steady stream past our wings on either side.It seemed a miracle not to be hit. The rapid descent of a dive-bombing run in our propeller-driven Spitfires caused constantly altering forces of torque as the speed increased. These required ever-changing control on the rudder to ensure that the bomb, when dropped, would fall in its desired path. This, together with the intensive concentration on the target, which was essential, meant that it was not until the flight was over that the menace of the enemy fire really sank into our consciousness. Then, in our minds, we relived the experience. With the comradeship and the good-humour of our fellow pilots we did our best to put these memories aside; but we knew that tomorrow there would be another sortie to be flown.

On one occasion, whilst attacking transport on a mountain road and encountering a hail of light anti-aircraft fire, I was struck in my port wing by a 40mm shell. The top surface of the wing was ballooned up by the explosion, strong fumes of burning cordite filled the cockpit and I was obliged to open the hood to clear the air. The distorted upper surface of the wing greatly reduced the lift on the port side and a lot of aileron control was needed to keep the wings level. I could not tell how much damage had been done to the internal structure of the wing but I knew that I must keep my speed down and handle the aircraft with the utmost gentleness. The other members of my flight shepherded me back to base. I was glad to have them alongside.

35

Back at the airfield, I was astonished to see the extent of the damage to the underside of the wing. There was little of it left and the main spar was found to be fractured. One of the shells in my own 20mm cannon magazine had been penetrated by shrapnel and the cordite within it had burnt out. How it did not explode and set off the whole magazine I shall never understand. That shell case sits now on my study shelf as a reminder of my good fortune.

One target I remember particularly was Figline, a vital communications centre south-east of Florence. Through the town, alongside each other, ran a road, a railway and a river or canal. We were targeted to dive-bomb a bridge, and light anti-aircraft fire saturated the air as we attacked. When, a few days later we were briefed to return to the dreaded Figline, to bomb a headquarters building, our feelings can be imagined; but, again, all four of us survived. Nevertheless, these forms of attack were particularly hazardous and many pilots from the Wing were lost.

# Chapter 4

# An Unwelcome Interlude (1944)

*For they that led us away captive required of us then a*
*song, and melody* – Psalm 137

After a short spell based at RAF Luqa in Malta, we rejoined *Attacker*
and sailed for the waters off the coast of southern France in support
of the landings on the beaches by the allied armies. Naval strength
was deployed on a massive scale. A total of no fewer than nine
aircraft carriers, seven from the Royal Navy and two from the
United States Navy, in two separate fleets, began operating some
70 miles off the coast on 15th August 1944. The carriers' task was
to provide air cover over the fleets and above the beaches, with
tactical and photographic reconnaissance and close support for the
troops ashore.

In the first phase of our operations we launched sorties continuously
from dawn to dusk for five days. It soon became apparent that the
Luftwaffe was either not able, or not willing, to take any significant
part in attacking the shipping offshore, or opposing the invading
troops as they established their beachhead and then moved inland.
Consequently our permanent fighter patrols over the fleets and above
the beaches were largely discontinued. Our work thereafter was
almost entirely devoted to tactical reconnaissance and photographic
reconnaissance and, following reports from these, to attacking the
enemy with cannon, rockets and bombs wherever they could be
found. We ranged far and wide on our reconnaissance flights over
the south of France. I flew always with George, who exercised his
remarkable skill at spotting the enemy on the ground. While he
concentrated his attention on the countryside beneath us, especially
on roads, railways, fields and woods, he relied on me to be on the

37

alert for any German fighters which might descend upon us. In the event no such attacks materialised and the only opposition we encountered was from enemy ground fire. The weather each day was fine but, as at Salerno the previous year, there was little or no natural wind, making deck-landing on our tiny, slow, escort carriers a renewed test of skill. Our ships, as they sailed over a glassy ocean, kept a full 24-hour alert, expecting enemy air attacks, but none came.

After five days of continuous operations we withdrew overnight to Maddalena, a secluded haven lying between Corsica and Sardinia. At first light we arrived at this peaceful anchorage to spend a few hours in rest and recuperation before returning to the French coast for another spell of ops. At the rock-bound and apparently unpopulated refuge of Maddalena we went ashore by the boatload accompanied by bounteous provision of food and drink to spend the daylight hours relaxing in good-humoured fellowship, luxuriating in the warm, clear water and, most of all, relishing the freedom from the limiting confines of our ship. At sundown we were once again on board, the anchor was weighed and *Attacker* sailed on her overnight passage back to the invasion coast and the carrier fleet.

Early on the following morning, 21st August, the seventh day of the invasion, I was programmed for the dawn sortie, a reconnaissance of the area between Nimes and Avignon. Our task was to look especially for enemy movement on the roads. Lieutenant George Ogilvy was my section leader. Between the two of us we hoped to find and report targets for other rocket-firing aircraft to attack. We took off just before sunrise and flew through clear skies to the coast. As the light increased, the sea sparkled in the early sunshine. It was a typical Mediterranean morning but, as we approached the land, we saw that the ground was obscured by fog and low cloud. Not long after we crossed the coast to begin our task we received a radio call from George Calder, another one of the pilots from our squadron, who was on a reconnaissance some distance to the east of us; he had been hit by anti-aircraft fire and was on his way down. This was distressing news to us as Calder was a close friend and, for me, a long-time 'running-ashore' mate. We continued our flight, hoping that the fog would clear as the sun warmed the air, but we found nothing to report in the next 30 minutes although, from time to time, we did fly over small areas which were clear of fog.

Our task seemed to be impossible so we decided to return to the ship, but no sooner had we set course than we flew over another small patch of countryside which was visible. We looked down and there, before our eyes, was a long column of motorised heavy artillery moving along a tree-lined road. The vehicles stopped as we approached and I was ordered down to strafe some guns and tractors which had pulled in behind the trees. Seeing no anti-aircraft fire, usually all too clearly visible to the attacking pilot, I ignored the 'one target – one attack' rule and made several firing runs on the column; but during the fourth attack my Seafire was hit in the engine. There was a heavy explosion and as I climbed away my windscreen became covered with oil, fumes filled the cockpit and white smoke poured from the exhaust stubs. The smoke soon became black as I struggled to gain altitude and I was lucky to reach about 4,000 feet before the engine burst into flames and then seized solid. I had already undone my straps and was all prepared to bale out.

We believed that there were just two ways to bale out of a Spitfire. After jettisoning the hood, one plan was to open the side door and try to throw oneself out through the opening, hoping not to be struck by the tailplane. The second plan was to invert the aircraft and fall out. I had decided that, if ever the need arose, I would use the second method.

It was recommended that, once free of the aircraft, one should 'stand to attention' in mid-air. This would stop the violent tumbling and so avoid the shroud lines becoming entangled with the legs when the parachute was deploying. We were advised always to look down to find the ripcord handle before pulling it. Horror stories circulated of airmen striking the ground before the chute opened because they had wasted time feeling for the handle instead of sighting it.

The flames quickly enveloped the cockpit and to get out was an easy decision to take. With my parting words to George 'My engine's going and so am I' I rolled the aircraft over with the intention of dropping out. Unfortunately I had lost all my airspeed in the steep climb to gain height and the nose dropped before I was fully inverted. I fell half clear, but my legs remained trapped in the cockpit as the aircraft dived towards the ground.

With all the strength I could muster I strained forward until the stick was just within reach. I gave it a flip with the backs of my fingers. The result was immediate and violent. I was literally ejected from the cockpit, to find myself tumbling over and over in a wild rush of air. After a few seconds everything calmed down and I pulled the ripcord. It came away so easily that I thought, for an unhappy moment, that it could not have worked properly. Then there was a sudden jerk and I was floating down in comfort with this huge canopy above me. During the descent I was surprised to feel no sensation of falling and, as I looked around, I heard my Seafire strike the ground with a numbing explosion. From a small village nearby I could see soldiers running in my direction. A shot rang out and, assuming that I was being fired at, I used the shroud lines to swing myself about, but no more shots followed.

There was just time to manoeuvre myself around to face the way I was drifting before suddenly, at the last moment, the land seemed to rush up at me at an alarming rate. Then I was on the ground and, although I had no previous experience of parachuting, my landing was safe, and in a grassy field. My arrival on land was painless and as soon as I touched down I unclipped my parachute and, bundling it up, ran into an area of scrub which bordered the field. My first action was to strip off my Mae West, remove the various escape aids which it contained, and bury it and the parachute in a nearby ditch which was conveniently full of leaves. Only then did I realise that my dinghy had become detached when I released myself from the parachute and that it was still lying in the open field where I had landed. Already I could hear the sounds of motorcycles moving towards me from the village, so in order to put as much distance as possible between me and my landing place, which unfortunately was now clearly marked by the dinghy, I began to run deeper into the scrub.

I had gone only a short distance when, hearing the shouts of men, I decided that I must take cover and hope for the best. I lay face down in the thickest bush I could find and in a matter of a few minutes the whole area was alive with searchers who, not content with shouting, were loosing off their rifles, presumably into the air, to scare me out. A party of soldiers passed so close to me that, had I stretched out an arm, I could have tripped them, but they did not see me. This encouraged me greatly, and as the shouts and footsteps faded into the distance I began to hope that I might avoid capture. Before long, however, I heard them returning, for clearly they knew I was somewhere in the scrub. This time they found me, and the general clamour rose in a crescendo round my bush. I lifted my head, half turned and found myself the aiming point of half a dozen rifles and surrounded by double that number of men. I carefully raised my hands above my head before I got up.

I was thoroughly searched and all my belongings, including my escape materials, were removed from me. They even examined my shoes and the lining of my battledress jacket, although they failed to find two small compasses which were concealed behind the breast pocket buttons.

I much resented the removal of my watch and, with the aid of signs, English, French and broken German, I indicated that they had no right to take it from me and that, if they did, I would speak to their officers about it. I was astounded when the *Feldwebel* (Sergeant) in charge of the search party ordered that the watch be returned to me at once.

We then marched off to the village, the streets of which were lined with interested spectators. We entered a walled compound and I was brought before the Company Commander, a *Hauptmann* (Captain). He was a slightly built man with cold eyes who began to shout at me in rapid German. I indicated to him, and to another officer present, that I did not understand him, and I repeatedly gave him my name and rank, which they noted down. They continued to interrogate me for some time and to each question I just shrugged my shoulders. Eventually, giving up, they looked at each other and shrugged theirs. With a parting burst of vituperation from the *Hauptmann* I was led away to spend the rest of the day under guard in a building forming one wall of the compound. I learnt later that I was in the village of Marguerittes, about four miles north-east of Nimes.

From the first moment of my capture my thoughts were continuously of my parents and family. I knew that I was all right but they, of course, would be stricken with doubts and suffering agonies of worry. As I sat alone in my locked room I realised that there was no friend anywhere in my life, not even a fellow prisoner to talk to. Everyone around me was an enemy. I was totally in their power and I had no idea what was to be done with me. The transformation of my life had been as complete as it had been sudden, and I was struck by an overwhelming feeling of loneliness.

41

During the day I was visited by the doctor. I was suffering no ill effects from my bale-out and parachute descent but, when asked if there was anything I particularly wanted, I replied that I would much appreciate a toothbrush as I had a most horrible taste in my mouth. When this simple request was refused I concluded that the doctor was no more human than the other officers, of whom I had already formed an unfavourable opinion.

In the early afternoon I was taken out to a Volkswagen. With a guard and one of the officers we set off along a country road. The German infantry company obviously wished to be rid of me and to transfer me to the nearest authority for prisoners of war. We had not gone half a mile before several allied aircraft appeared overhead and forced us to take cover. The aircraft flew off, but no sooner had we resumed our journey than more appeared and we again had to abandon the vehicle and take cover in a nearby trench. The officer then decided that it was not worth risking the almost certain destruction of his transport just to get me off his hands, so we returned as fast as possible to our starting point, where I was again locked up.

When it began to get dark the Germans assembled their column, which consisted of about 20 horse-drawn vehicles, a Volkswagen for the *Hauptmann*, a small French car for the doctor and the vet, a lorry of about 30 hundredweight for the *Oberleutnant*, or second-in-command, and for me. They bundled me into the back and rather thoughtfully threw in a mattress on top of some drums of petrol, the contents of which as far as I could gather had to get them to the Siegfried Line, petrol supplies en route being somewhat unreliable.

My captors, I found out later, were one of the rifle companies of an infantry battalion forming part of 198 Division. They had not been in action in this particular battle as they had been stationed to the west of the area of the landings. Further, instead of being thrown into the breach they had been given orders to retreat up the Rhône Valley whilst escape was still possible. Thus it was that I found myself remaining in the company of my original captors for the long trip to Germany.

We trundled off along the darkening roads towards the north and I lay down on my mattress and began to think of how I might escape from the vehicle without the knowledge of the two guards who were stationed at the tail board. During the 18 months that I had been on operations I had attended a number of lectures which emphasised the prisoner's duty to escape. We were given helpful guidance on how we might set about it, with a number of proven 'do's and don'ts' to consider in the process. The stories of successful escapes which were recounted during these talks were always of riveting interest and they gave great encouragement. I knew that my chances of escape were at their best while I was being moved to a camp but that, once inside one, they would be very much reduced. The strain of the day's events, however, proved too much for me, the effort of concentration was too great, and soon I fell asleep. When I awoke it was daylight and there was nothing to be done but curse myself for letting sleep get the better of me.

On this day, 22nd August, and D-Day plus seven, I passed the time in a farmhouse still occupied by a French family. The German company and all their transport were assembled in the large farmyard surrounded by high barns. I was shut up in one of the bedrooms under guard but I managed to speak to the daughter of the house when she brought food, and she promised to pass my name to the American Army, whose advance apparently was continuing. I was most anxious that word of my safety should reach my family as soon as possible and, since neither of my guards spoke French, I was fortunate to be able to have a short conversation with the young lady.

That evening I was again put into the lorry and we were on the move at dusk. By this time I was ready to go to work on a scheme for getting out of this nightly prison on wheels. It had a canvas hood which was strapped down to the outside of the side boards in a number of places. Running fore-and-aft inside the canvas hood, and attached to the main steel frames, were longitudinal wooden slats spaced about eight inches apart. One of these, however, and fortunately the one immediately above the left-hand side board, had been broken and a small part of it was missing. There was thus a narrow gap about 18 inches deep above the top of the left side board and the lowest slat. As I lay on my mattress, comfortably wedged into the V-shape between two petrol drums, my head was next to the top of the left side board and my feet stretched towards the other side. When I lay on my right side I faced the tail board and I could see the guards silhouetted against the night sky. With my left arm crooked and my head on my left hand I was able to get my right arm through the gap made by the broken slat and move my hand along the outside of the side board without the guards seeing what I was doing, even when they shone a torch on me, which they did at frequent intervals. I managed to get one strap of the canvas hood undone that night, but only after a lengthy struggle. Try as I could I found it impossible to reach the next one, which it would be necessary to undo before the canvas could be pushed out far enough to allow me to squeeze through. A mass of branches secured to the canvas for camouflage made the task of undoing the straps more difficult.

So the next day came, 23rd August, and we hid up in a wooded area near a small village. It was indeed an education to see the troops conceal themselves. Directly they arrived at a suitable bivouac area, which was usually wooded and off a side road, the horses were tethered under the trees and then all hands got to work cutting branches to camouflage the wagons. The job was soon complete and so thorough that, from even a short distance, the vehicles resembled bushes. It was obviously out of the question to move the horses by day because of the chaos that would ensue from air attack, and the few columns that I did see on the roads by day were fully mechanised and generally contained artillery.

I spent the day lying in the shade of the trees, chatting as best I could with my guards and to other soldiers. The majority spoke neither French nor English; nevertheless, I found it a simple matter to make myself understood by a combination of signs and various mixed languages. The one year of German I had done at school stood me in good stead. I found no difficulty in keeping on good terms with some of the soldiers, particularly the older ones, but the young ones I classed with the officers as being basically anti-human and thus to be avoided as much as possible. They all assumed that I was an RAF pilot who had flown over from Corsica, and they had no knowledge of the presence of aircraft carriers supporting the landings. What they did know was that the sky was often unpleasantly filled with the sound of allied aircraft. The fact that the majority were naval aircraft from the force of nine carriers steaming off the coast was of no consequence to them, but it was the sight of these planes overhead, flown by my friends who still enjoyed their freedom, that gave me my worst moments of depression. At the same time I often felt it was most fortunate for me that I had been able to get some miles away from the German artillery column I had been attacking, and that it was not they who had captured me. The effect of the constant air attacks by our carrier aircraft was clearly indicated by the enormous number of damaged and burnt-out vehicles which lay abandoned along every road on which we travelled.

Instead of setting out at dusk as on previous days, we moved off during the afternoon and, before I was ordered to climb in, I had an opportunity to examine the lorry from the outside. Firstly, I saw that the strap which I had undone the night before was still undone. It was hidden by the camouflaging brushwood attached to the outside of the truck and had not been noticed. Secondly, I noted the position of a wooden tool box screwed to the body of the vehicle. It seemed that it would make a convenient foot rest for me should I succeed in my plan to squeeze out through the canvas. I decided that in order to do this it would be necessary to undo only one more strap, and I made a mental note of the position of the one most suitably placed. As the vehicles were loaded and the column assembled I noticed that my dinghy pack was thrown into my truck, instead of another wagon as on previous nights. I took this to be a good omen and decided that after dark I would somehow remove from it the escape aids, money and rations which the Germans had taken from me when I was first captured, and stored in the pack. If I could escape I would then be as well equipped as I had been on my arrival in France by parachute.

We had been going for only about half an hour when the column stopped and I heard the drone of aircraft engines. We all immediately abandoned the truck and I was pushed into a nearby slit trench, one of many which lined every road along which the Germans travelled. From the trench I could see eight Hellcats circling high above us: obviously my friends from the carrier force. I felt certain that our transport was to be their target. My luck was in, however, for they discovered a more attractive convoy on a road parallel to ours a few miles off. We watched them dive and pull away, leaving several soaring plumes of black smoke behind them. My guards followed the attack and looked at me with displeasure, as they always did when our planes were about. I smiled back and mentally wished our boys good hunting.

On emerging from the trenches we found we had stopped right beside a large French van which had been abandoned by the roadside. It was piled high inside with the multitude of things that might be found in a provincial general store. Once this was discovered there was an immediate rush on it by everyone except my two guards, who got back into the lorry with me. Every soldier took something and there were two French women there helping themselves to dresses. Thanks to the thoughtfulness of one soldier who had been friendly to me, I benefited as well to the extent of a complete razor set with spare blades, soap, toothbrush and toothpaste, all of which he knew I needed. I was particularly pleased with the razor since I was anxious to remove my beard, carefully nurtured over the past two months, but which I now felt made me too conspicuous.

My other acquisition was a violin in a case, and on this I contrived a passable rendition of 'Lili Marlene', which the Germans were very surprised to find that I knew. They were unaware that this famous song, which had originated in Germany and was 'top-of-the-pops' with the Afrika Korps had, because of its charm and sentimentality, been adopted by the British and was likewise 'top-of-the-pops' with our armed forces all over the world. Again, two years of violin lessons at school had stood me in good stead and did no harm at all to my standing with the infantry soldiers who were my captors. I think that they were delighted. My guards explained that the van had probably been owned by collaborators who, driving north with the contents of their shop to avoid the retribution coming to them, had fallen prey to a party of Maquis. They had, doubtless, suffered the fate they deserved.

Once again we set off, but it was discouraging to find three extra soldiers in the back of the lorry. Previously there had been only the two guards and one other soldier accompanying me, with the *Oberleutnant* and the driver in front. Now with a total of seven Germans in the truck, I did not fancy my chances of getting out undetected however dark the night. During the long wait for darkness to fall I moved to a position where I would be able most easily to reach the second strap, and there I sat, carefully running through my plans. When eventually it became really dark I set to work and, within a few minutes, I had undone the strap and convinced myself that I could push out the canvas far enough for me to squeeze through, although the brushwood on the outside would make it difficult. Shortly afterwards we made a stop at a farm, where we had a mug of coffee while waiting for the horse-drawn transport to catch up and pass us. As I was the first person back into the lorry after the halt, it was a simple matter for me to push the dinghy pack to the far corner where previously I had been sitting. In no time at all I opened the pack and stuffed my pockets with preserved rations, maps, money and knife. As we drove off again I was delighted to find that two of the extra soldiers had left us and that there were now only the two guards and one other with me in the back. Shortly after we resumed our journey this extra man lay down, and soon he obligingly fell asleep.

I was sure that, if ever there was a right time for getting out of the lorry, that time had arrived. I was satisfied enough with my plan but at the last moment I felt a powerful reluctance to carry it out. This was the 'moment of truth' and I had to summon up all the resolution I could muster to make the final effort. I decided that, to give myself the maximum head start should my attempt be successful, I would climb out as soon as possible after the guards next shone their torch on me.

For this I had not long to wait, and as the beam of light faded I pushed out the canvas hood and slid my left leg over the side board and out through the gap. With my foot I felt for and found the tool box. Letting it take my weight, I half turned inwards and manoeuvred my other leg out to join the first. I was then left standing on the tool box with my body still inside the truck. Gently pushing my back outwards whilst bending forward at the waist, and making as little noise as possible, I eased down until I was completely outside the canvas and clinging to the side of the lorry just behind the cab, in which the driver, most reassuringly, continued to drive on through the night. I clung on for a few moments and then, as the truck slowed to go round a corner, I flung myself headlong into the ditch and lay still. My most apprehensive moment became my most exhilarating as the lorry rumbled on and disappeared into the darkness. When the noise of the engine faded into the distance I picked myself up and moved off the roadside into some trees.


I had no knowledge of where I was but I estimated that for the past three nights I had travelled roughly north at perhaps 25 or 30 miles a night. What I did know for certain was that to lessen my chances of recapture, I must get as far away from my present position as possible. So to solve the problem temporarily I brought out my miniature compass, studied it, and struck south.

The confidence with which I started my walk soon evaporated as I encountered one obstacle after another. I had constantly to retrace my steps because I ran into marshland and, in trying to find detours, I plunged time and again into large clumps of thick bushes. My progress was hopelessly slow and after an hour or two I decided to give up walking that night, as soon as I could find somewhere secure to hide up for the next day, when I would have a chance to study the local countryside.

Everything was silent as I was walking along, with a wood on my right and an open field, bordered by another wood, on my left. Suddenly I heard a gentle clanging sound coming towards me which I decided must be a cow with a bell round its neck but, as it came nearer, my straining eyes made out the figure of a man. I immediately froze under a tree I was passing, but he had seen me and just before he drew level with me he slowed his pace. Then with his eyes fixed on me – almost, I thought, in a scared way – he literally sidled past me and was gone. As he passed I saw that he was a soldier and that it was the mess tins attached to his belt that were making the bell-like clatter. This experience unnerved me and I rushed blindly across the field and crashed headlong into the wood, tearing my clothes on bramble thickets and certainly making a great deal of noise. When I recovered from this regrettable bout of panic I lay still for a long time, listening for signs of the search for me that I felt must inevitably be under way, but all remained quiet. My heart was beating so hard and loudly that I feared that its thumping noise must be audible to any searchers. I concluded that the soldier must have thought me to be a member of the Maquis and I gave thanks for the terror in which they were held by the Germans.

This encounter confirmed my decision to find a hiding place without delay and I set off with added caution, determined to lie up in the first large open space I could find. I had been with the Germans long enough to know that they spent the daylight hours in the shelter of woods or towns, so I had made up my mind that the safest place to hide was an open field where there was long grass to protect me from view. I soon came upon a field which, in the darkness, appeared ideal for my purpose. It contained just a few scattered bushes and plenty of long grass. In this I settled down to spend the remainder of the night.

After a short and fitful sleep I awoke with the early morning light and peered cautiously out from my hiding place, for I heard some movement on a nearby road. Passing along it was a column of what appeared to be Bofors guns towed by horses. I watched them for a while, feeling quite secure in my hideout, then, to my dismay, one of them turned into the field – my field! It was followed by several more, together with some wagons, and, as I crouched lower and lower in the grass, I watched them position the guns along two sides of the field and unhitch the horses. The wagons were driven up to the bushes, which the soldiers then cut for camouflage. I lay down on my back, cursing my poor fortune, as one wagon approached so close to me that I could see the horses' heads towering above me. I was still not observed but the suspense was intense, and the prospect of spending all day with the enemy in such close proximity was almost unbearable. There was great activity on all sides and it became obvious to me that sooner or later I was bound to be discovered by one of the many soldiers who were swarming over the field.

Then it happened. A soldier, apparently walking across the field in a casual manner, literally walked on top of me. He gave the alarm and I was surrounded even before I could rise from the ground. I was taken to a young officer who, after questioning me in French, which he spoke well, arranged for me to have some breakfast. I was chilled after a night in the open and dispirited at my recapture but the two pieces of black bread and the mug of hot ersatz coffee went some way to revive my morale. My recapture I could put down only to the most outrageous bad luck. I felt I could not pin blame on myself for any action I had taken, except the panic after meeting the soldier during the previous night, and that seemed not to have had any bearing on subsequent events. My escape had proceeded with a success beyond all my hopes, and my short-lived high spirits sank low at being so soon returned to captivity. That I was caught by a German unit that was not even searching for me was particularly galling.

As I sat eating my bread, the reason the Germans had chosen this position for the siting of their guns became apparent. Quite unknowingly I had spent the night not more than a hundred yards from the bank of a large river, at a point half a mile or so upstream from a big suspension bridge. This bridge had been destroyed, presumably by bombing, and to replace it the Germans had set up a ferry crossing operated by two double pontoon rafts, each with a large outboard motor at the stern. The ferries were already running across the river at a point slightly upstream from where I was sitting. The battery which had occupied my field was to provide anti-aircraft protection for them throughout the day. Again I was impressed by the way the troops concealed themselves and their weapons. The guns of the battery sited along the river bank and across one end of the field were already completely hidden beneath cut brushwood, and the wagons and horses were dispersed in a nearby wood.

I sat for some time on the river bank watching the busy scene around me. Men and transport were crossing the river as fast as the two ferries could carry them, and as one group after another embarked on the flat raft-like boats, they were replaced by others which emerged from the wood. Several times I spotted allied aircraft high overhead and I thought of the havoc that would ensue if they discovered the mass of men and equipment concealed in that wood, but they paid no attention to us. Later I was escorted along the river bank in the direction of the ferries, and towards a group of three men who were obviously waiting for me. One was the young officer who had given me breakfast. The other – the one man I hoped above all others never to see again – was the *Hauptmann* of the company from which I had so recently escaped.

As I approached I felt that at that moment my fate hung in the balance. I knew that the American advance was continuing and that the Germans were so harassed from the air that road movement of any sort by day was fraught with danger – that they were, in fact, under maximum pressure. I was not sure that their patience could be stretched very far at any time but, under these circumstances, I was extremely apprehensive about the measures the *Hauptmann* might take to punish me for the trouble I had caused him the previous night. As I was handed over to him he seemed literally speechless with rage, particularly when all the maps, money and other escape aids which his unit had confiscated from me when I was first captured, and of which I had again taken possession before my escape, were handed over to him by my escort from the AA Gunners.

My fears for my immediate safety were groundless, however, for after a few moments of silence he rapped out the word '*Marsch!*' and we set off for the ferry. Arriving there, I was handed over to two new guards whom I had not met before and we stood waiting our turn to cross the river. Whilst idling thus, I had time to spare a thought of sympathy for my guards of previous days, who had shown me kindness and who were now, doubtless, paying in some way for allowing me to take advantage of them. I felt a sincere, if illogical, pang of sorrow for them and a strong sense of shame at myself for being captured again so soon. I never saw those soldiers again or, for that matter, any other familiar faces amongst the new group with whom I travelled.

Our crossing of the river, which took place about mid-morning, went off without incident, and our next move took us on foot a few miles up a valley leading north-east from the river until, finally, we found a suitable area in which to pass the remainder of the day. My two new guards, one a corporal and the other a private, spent the whole day with me. They were complete opposites in character. The corporal, a round, bouncing little man with a ruddy complexion, was relaxed, ready to talk and friendly. The other, younger, man was of sour demeanour; when he had to speak to me, he did so by shouting and he took every opportunity to jab his rifle in my back whenever he escorted me anywhere. His looks and behaviour were, I thought, those of a typical young Nazi.

It was a long walk and, as it was a hot day, I was extremely thirsty and wished to ask for water at a cottage we were passing. The young guard was adamantly opposed to this, but the corporal overruled him, though angry words passed between them. I got my water.

That evening, when we got on the move I found myself no longer lying in comfort on my mattress in the back of the lorry but, instead, wedged between the driver and the corporal on the hard bench seat of one of the wagons. Despite the discomfort I was profoundly thankful that it was the corporal and not the young soldier who was guarding me. We had been going for less than half and hour when he warned me that I would be shot if I made another attempt to escape, but he made it clear that he would much regret it if that happened. He might have saved his breath, though, for I was so disgusted with my luck on the previous night that I had no thoughts or plans for another attempt so soon afterwards. The road was a bumpy one, and as it grew dark it became cold. I was still wearing a battledress jacket but my thin khaki trousers and shirt, already torn by the brambles I had blundered into the night before, offered little protection. The corporal, however, produced from the wagon a beautiful blue eiderdown, a trophy from some French home, with which he covered himself. When I pulled part of it over me he made no objection. To outer comfort he then added inner warmth in the form of cognac, which he offered me from his water bottle. Here was a soldier who really knew how to make the best of things and who was generous to boot, and some of my depression began to leave me as we plodded on through the night. The column of wagons, each towed by a pair of powerful horses, moved in complete darkness, without a light of any kind on the vehicles. The only illumination was provided by the men occasionally switching on dimmed red or blue torches attached to their tunics.

The cramped conditions in which we travelled and the hardness of the seat made sleep impossible and during the long hours of the night I talked continually to the corporal, whose name I found was Konrad. The task of conversing in a mixture of languages, and with signs when all else failed, fascinated me and I was constantly amazed at the ease with which I could understand the German soldiers, and they me. Konrad told me of his wife, whom he had not seen for over two years, and from whom he rarely had a letter due to the chaotic transport conditions in France. He had been in the army since the beginning of the war, three years of which he had spent on the Eastern front. His experiences there had been ghastly and it was clear that he was heartily sick of the war. He spoke especially of the fearsome weather conditions which the German troops had suffered during the freezing winters in the Caucasus, and of the inadequate equipment and clothing with which they were supplied. He seemed delighted to be fighting the British and Americans instead of the Russians, of whom he stood in obvious terror. He clearly felt that although Germany might hold out for a long time, she was doomed to eventual defeat by the combined forces of East and West. He had no illusions that Hitler was a superior being who could turn the tide of defeat into victory. So we talked on until, by the end of the night, I felt I was on terms of firm friendship with this veteran corporal. Finally, just as the sun was rising, the column halted under the cover of trees and preparations for breakfast began. This meal consisted, as always, of a small tin of cold meat, two slices of hard black bread and a cup of ersatz coffee.

After breakfast I decided to shave off my beard. There seemed no point in being more conspicuous than necessary but, on the other hand, I thought the *Hauptmann* might be suspicious if I suddenly removed it. Anyway, off it came with the aid of scissors, water and razor, all of which Konrad produced for me. I felt much refreshed as a result, although I regretted that the Germans had led me to take a step which the Captain of my ship, HMS *Attacker*, who disapproved of beards, had failed to persuade me to take. Afterwards I lay down on the ground, pulled Konrad's blue eiderdown over me and enjoyed my first undisturbed sleep in three days.

I awoke at noon in time for the only hot meal of the day which, as usual, consisted of a hotchpotch of vegetables with a few chunks of meat thrown in for luck. A sort of lard was provided to spread on the bread and each soldier received a daily ration of a small tin containing two rounds of plain chocolate. The vines in the many vineyards through which we passed were loaded with ripe grapes, so we were never short of fresh fruit. After the meal Konrad told me that he had been ordered to take me into the nearby town of Grignan and to hand me over to the divisional headquarters for further interrogation and disposal. This news filled me with gloom for, although I knew it was inevitable that I should be transferred sooner or later, I dreaded the moment and I knew that my chances of escape would be greatly reduced once I was in the hands of the proper organisation for prisoners of war. As long as I was with the field unit I felt there might always be opportunities to escape, for it had a multitude of problems on its hands besides me.

We set off to walk the few miles into Grignan. No sound of war marred that afternoon. Only the incessant chirruping song of crickets filled the air. The German army slept in the woods and fields, resting before another hectic night of retreat towards their homeland. We walked the dusty roads through bursting vineyards and the land was totally still in the shimmering heat of the sun. The boots of my guards tramped heavily behind me and I felt depressed at the unknown prospect ahead.

The scene in Grignan was in marked contrast. The town was packed with German troops and with transport of every kind, ranging from motor cycles to armoured cars. General confusion reigned throughout the narrow streets, which were so solidly jammed with soldiers and vehicles that it was scarcely possible to make headway, even on foot.

We stopped amid a throng of soldiers and Konrad, having ordered

53

me to sit down on the pavement, despatched the young Nazi guard to search for the divisional headquarters. As I sat there I found myself the object of very considerable interest. The soldiers clustered round me, laughing at me and joking. They were obviously enjoying my discomfiture. This was a most unpleasant experience but, after a while, they grew accustomed to me and left me alone, for which I was thankful. Konrad sat down next to me and we talked away to pass the time. I had by now become quite expert at making myself understood by a curious mixture of languages and signs.

I suggested to him that as both he and I had had enough of the war this was an ideal opportunity for us to 'disappear' and make our way undetected to join the Americans. I told him that if he helped me to get away he would not be made a prisoner of war but would be sent to the USA or Canada to work on a farm, where he would be treated virtually as a free man. He made no reply to my proposition and I was not sure that he had understood me. Shortly afterwards the young guard returned, having apparently failed to locate the headquarters. Konrad then set off himself, after instructing the Nazi to remain with me. He was away for a long time and my guard permitted me to sit in a nearby barber's shop, instead of on the pavement.

Eventually Konrad returned and gave some instructions to the other guard, who then departed, leaving the corporal and me in the barber's shop. The time passed slowly as I watched soldier after soldier having his 'short-back-and-sides', which must have been a requirement for German troops no less than for our servicemen. After a wait of some hours we were joined by another soldier, a stranger to me. He spoke to Konrad, who then instructed me to stand up and leave the shop. We walked back along the main street in the direction from which we had entered the town, and then turned off down a minor side road. We soon left the crowds and confusion behind us and found ourselves in a quiet part of the town where only French civilians were to be seen. We came upon a narrow, rutted cul-de-sac between two rows of stone houses and, entering it, we proceeded to the shelter of a disued building. Here Konrad and his companion had a lengthy discussion, at the conclusion of which they seemed to have reached a decision. They then questioned me at length about the treatment they would receive from the Americans should they be made prisoners of war. I repeated my previous assurances that they would be treated most favourably,

54

and would almost certainly be shipped to the United States or Canada to work on the land in virtual freedom until the end of the war.

I could scarcely believe my ears when, after further discussion between themselves, they told me that they intended to join forces with me and that, together, the three of us would make our way to the allied armies, which they estimated were not more than 40 miles away. We first decided that we would wait until dark and then venture out across country, but later my two friends concluded that to try and walk south to penetrate the lines of both sides would be too dangerous and that we had a better chance of achieving our objective if we hid up and waited for the American advance to overtake us. I had complete faith in the judgement of this veteran corporal who, after several years of active service, much of it on the Eastern front must, I felt, know just about everything there was to know about moving around on foot in a battle zone. My own experience of trying to walk at night through strange country infested with troops confirmed the soundness of our decision, but the problem of where to hide worried us a great deal.

Eventually we decided to seek assistance from the French. Here I drew again upon advice given in the aircrew lectures on how best to obtain help from the civil population of the Occupied countries. The first point to remember was to seek help from one person alone. If a party of two or more persons was approached, even though each individual might be anxious to help, they would never admit it in front of the others. Secondly, it was thought to be a mistake to approach any well-dressed or prosperous-looking person. A poor person was more likely to be imbued with the milk of human kindness. Thirdly, experience had shown that women were more often willing to give help than men. Thus the obvious thing to do seemed to be to wait in the shelter of our building until a poorly dressed lone female appeared; then, if she looked the helpful type, I would approach her. We did not have long to wait before such a lady came near to our hiding place; I emerged from the building and, in the best French I could manage, explained my situation. This was the nerve-jangling and testing moment when betrayal or help were equal possibilities. Despite the unlikely story that I gave her, and I must confess that I myself found it hard to believe, she said she would speak to a friend and return as soon as possible. The afternoon was by this time well advanced, but before dark she was back again with another woman who, after questioning me further and taking a look at the Germans, showed us through a broken grating into an old cellar. She told us to remain there until nightfall, when she would return.

After dark the two women reappeared and led us to a more secure hiding place. This was an unoccupied and derelict house which could be approached only by a footpath. The floor had fallen through into the cellar in several places and part of the house had no roof. It was thus totally uninhabitable and clearly ideal for our purpose. We settled down on a pile of dirty straw in a corner and made a meal of some food which the women had brought us. Then they insisted that I should go with them to meet the 'Resistance Chief', but that the Germans must remain where they were. Konrad and his friend, whose name was Kurt, were most reluctant to let me out of their sight but, since the women refused to take them along as well, they had little option but to let me go. I gave them the most solemn promise to return and sealed this assurance with hand-on-heart and handshakes all round.

We walked in darkness through narrow alleyways to the house of the 'Chief', who turned out to be the husband of the second woman. There I was made comfortable in the parlour and, whilst being plied with coffee, nuts and liqueurs, I told my story. How thankful I was for the years of French lessons I had enjoyed at school. The Frenchman and his wife were naturally very suspicious of the two Germans, but they agreed that we should stay in our hide-out until the following day, when an interpreter would be brought there to question them. After an hour or so of their pleasant company I was returned to the Germans for the night. I believe that they were extremely relieved to see me. Whilst they sat alone in our shelter during the hours that I was away, they must have suffered agonies of doubt as to whether the decision to put their fate in the hands of the French had been a wise one. They knew of the brutal atrocities which had been carried out by the Gestapo in the south of France. They knew that hostages had been taken, tortured and shot in response to the actions of French patriots. They knew that there was no love for them amongst the local population and they must have wondered, too, whether I might betray them by breaking my promise and abandoning them to retribution at the hands of the Maquis. When I returned to them their relief was evident and they gave me the warmest of welcomes. I lay down on my pile of grubby straw. It was as good a bed as any I had known. As I dozed off to sleep I cast my thoughts back over the day's events and could hardly believe the amazing turn that my fortunes had taken.

The next day, 26th August, dawned after a restless night, during which there was constant and noisy activity through the town. As was usual during the hours of darkness, the German columns were all on the move. Several times we heard heavy explosions in the neighbourhood which we presumed were caused by demolitions. During the morning the Chief appeared with another Frenchman, who spoke fluent German and, after lengthy interrogation of Konrad and Kurt, pronounced himself satisfied that their stated intentions were genuine. The Chief then approved of our staying together under his care, but he made it clear that from then onwards we were to put ourselves entirely in his hands and carry out his orders implicitly.

At first the Chief intented to move us, but later he decided that the American advance was continuing so rapidly that it would be pointless to do so. We therefore stayed where we were and enjoyed the food and wine which were brought to us before dawn and after dusk each day. We were, in fact, grossly overeating and we must have been given many of the things which had been saved up for the great day of Liberation. Sometimes we simply could not eat all that we were given and then, to avoid giving offence to our hosts, we hid the surplus.

# Chapter 5

# *Freedom (1944)*

One afternoon shells began to whine over and fall around the town. I felt this must be another 'El Alamein' bombardment, but the two Germans assured me it was nothing, and they laughed at me as I cringed in my corner. Then, later on, the wife of the Chief rushed in to tell us that American troops had reached the outskirts of the town, and she advised us to go to her house for the night. She had brought civilian clothes for the two Germans. After they had changed into these and I had removed my battledress jacket we followed her home. She told us that there were only about 30 Germans left in the town, and that they were mostly snipers and machine gunners who were already in their defence positions with two radio vans for communications. We reached the house without incident and descended into a neighbouring cellar owned by a Madame Garcin. There we sat around in hushed expectancy, waiting for the battle to commence.

For the next three hours pandemonium reigned. All around us was the stutter and scream of rifle and machine gun fire, mixed with the explosions of grenades and mortars. Inside the cellar there was a continuous babble of excited voices of the many women and children who were sheltering with us. Finally, this nightmare came to an end and we heard that the town was clear. We all embraced each other wildly.

It was a thrilling experience to be with these French townsfolk on the day when they regained their freedom. That evening we all sat down to a special 'Liberation' dinner, with everything that had been saved for this longed-for occasion. I felt proud to share in the celebrations for which these simple and courageous people had waited for so many years. It was indeed an exciting evening for everyone and the pastis, anisette and wine flowed freely. As my French improved with every glass, I was able to express my heartfelt thanks to the Chief, whose name was Maurice, and to his wife, Madeleine. In their home that night, as I lay on a comfortable bed and between clean sheets, I could hardly believe that it was little more than a week since I had last slept in similar comfort on board HMS *Attacker*, the night before I was shot down.

The next morning I was taken on a tour of the town and to pay my respects to the Mayor, who was throwing a party. When finally I extracted myself from this, which was no easy matter, I went into the street and approached the first American officer I could find. I explained who I was and asked him what I should do with my two ex-guards who were still under cover in the Chief's house. He replied that they must be taken to the prisoner-of-war cage and that he and another officer would come and collect them.

We went together to the house but, before Konrad and Kurt were to be taken away, the Americans joined us all in a hilarious international luncheon party which surely must be remembered by all those who were present; for round the table in mutual celebration sat four French civilians, two American army officers, two German soldiers and one British naval officer. All of us, except our hosts, were wearing uniform and, although another year of war lay ahead, it was for us one isolated day of peace.

After lunch the Americans told me that they could not spare anyone to take the Germans to the cage and that I, therefore, must accompany them, though a jeep and driver would be provided. I felt badly about this and tried to persuade them to do the job themselves but they were adamant. It was reported that every one of the German defenders had been killed in the battle for Grignan on the previous day. Now, on the day of liberation, the town, after years of enemy occupation, was again under the control of its own citizens, and everyone seemed to be out in the streets enjoying the wonderful air of joyful celebration. Although I myself had not suffered the long months of subjugation that they had, I felt justified in joining these happy folk and revelling in my own new-found freedom. It was an experience never to be forgotten.

For Konrad and Kurt I wrote a note each to say that they had enabled me to escape, and that I hoped that they would receive favourable treatment. I added my own home address in the hope

60

that I might hear how they fared in the future. Ever since those days I have regretted that I did not make a note of the names and addresses of the two United States Army officers who joined our luncheon party at Maurice and Madeleine's home in Grignan, and who set me off on the journey back to my squadron. How I wish I had done so and thus been able to find out if they survived the rest of the war. Sadly, too, no photographs were taken of the celebrations in which I participated.

In the afternoon we took leave of the kindly folk of Grignan, amidst tears of farewell. I saw Konrad and Kurt safely behind the barbed wire of the prisoner-of-war cage, with more than a little feeling of guilt as I did so. Wearing Konrad's army belt round my waist and his P38 automatic pistol in its holster, I waved goodbye to my two friends and set off for the coast and the first leg of the journey to rejoin my ship.

I travelled in a convoy of American open-backed trucks carrying German prisoners. They were crammed in 60 to a truck, with two guards in the back and one with me and the driver in front. At every town and village through which we passed the Germans were assailed by stones and any other convenient missiles, hurled at them by vengeful French citizens. We stopped in one town square, where I disembarked to stretch my legs. It was a very hot day and many Germans passed down to me their water bottles, which I agreed to fill at the fountain. When the throng of French men and women saw what I was about to do they surrounded me in angry fashion and would not permit me to approach the water.

At an isolated spot in open countryside the convoy stopped. The driver and soldier in the front of our truck lifted the hinged lid of the bench seat on which we had been sitting. I saw that, inside, it was packed solid with cartons of cigarettes of assorted brands. The prisoners in the back were then stripped of all their private possessions – watches, rings, money; anything of value. In return for each item they received a few cigarettes. This episode shocked and disgusted me as I realised that this sort of thing must be going on everywhere behind the lines. These were not the troops who were doing the fighting but those who followed up behind the armies as support and transport forces. I wondered if the British Army support troops did the same. How ironic that the fighting soldiers risked their lives whilst the support troops feathered their nests. I was aware how fortunate I had been to be

61

captured and held by real veteran soldiers when I myself had been a prisoner. They, who knew what battle was, had treated me honourably.

On the two-day journey to the coast I enjoyed the good hot meals provided by the US Army and was given a tent to pass the night. The abundance of candy bars and other luxuries which were available right up to the front line had astonished me ever since I was freed in Grignan.

Gratitude to Madeleine and Maurice Tailland, my chief helpers in Grignan, has been a factor in my life ever since those stirring days. Maurice died at a rather young age but I have maintained a long friendship with Madeleine. She has stayed with me and my family in Britain and we have visited her on many occasions in the South of France. One of her granddaughters spent a summer holiday with us and we maintain contact to this day.

I believe that no stronger or more lasting bonds of friendship could be forged than between a wartime escaper and his helpers. These courageous citizens of an occupied country risked their lives to hide him from a brutal enemy and to give him succour in time of need. I was fortunate indeed to receive such help, and my feelings of thankfulness are deep and enduring. The lady whom I had first approached, Charlotte Bourmas, faded into the background after Maurice and Madeleine took over. When I tried to find her later I had no success, and I was unable to meet her to express my thanks and to say goodbye, but I remember her, too, with gratitude.

On arrival at St Tropez I was taken out to the headquarters ship, USS *Cotoctin*. There I was interviewed by Air Commodore Tuttle, who was interested in my story. He congratulated me on my two escapes from captivity and, in doing so, on reducing the Wehrmacht by another two soldiers. He told me that I was now entitled to two months' leave at home; news that delighted me. First, however, I must report to Mediterranean Command HQ for a thorough de-briefing and he made arrangements for me to be transported to Naples. The US Air Force flew me there the next day in a Mitchell light bomber. At Naples I was accommodated in a hotel and given a complete set of khaki tropical kit. My own clothing, torn, grubby and lice-ridden from the dirty straw in the hiding place at Grignan, was destroyed. How wonderful it was to have a bath and later, at an Italian hairdresser's, to be restored to some sort of presentability.

At the headquarters in the magnificent Caserta Palace I was given a thorough interrogation. Every detail of my experience was examined and the names and addresses of all my helpers were recorded.

During several days in Naples I was joined by George Calder and Gwynn Thomas, both of whom had been shot down over France but had succeeded in avoiding capture by the enemy. They had been able to hide up until they were overrun by the allied armies. George was a close friend of mine from my own squadron who had, in fact, been shot down on the same day as me. Gwynn was from 807 Squadron, attached to another carrier, and was not so well known to me but our reunion was a great joy, and recounting our experiences occupied many hours in the hotel bar.

From Naples we were flown to Alexandria, where our carriers were lying. The aircraft was an RAF Baltimore light bomber and we three passengers were accommodated in a blister on the underside of the fuselage. We spent a night at Bari on the coast of south-east Italy and continued our journey to Alex the following day, stopping at Malta and Derna in Libya on the way. For the last leg of the day the pilot had miscalculated the time of sunset at Alex and when we arrived it was pitch dark. The airfield there had no night flying facilities but, because we had insufficient fuel to divert to Cairo, there was no option but to land in total darkness. The pilot was familiar with the location of the airfield, but since no runways were visible, our arrival was to be a matter of faith and blind hope. We in the back knew of the situation but could do nothing but pray. After three abortive approaches, each followed by the desperate application of full power to climb away, the state of our nerves can perhaps be imagined. On the fourth attempt we struck the ground, careered across the airfield, through the boundary fence and over a sunken road. On the far side the nose dug in and we made a complete somersault. The overturned bomber was lying on its back. I don't know how long it was before rescuers came to release us from the wreckage but the three of us in the blister were unhurt, though shaken up. The pilot unfortunately was very badly injured and was carried off to hospital. After all our fraught experiences of the past weeks this seemed the last straw.

The captain of the *Attacker*, Harold Farncombe, gave me a warm welcome when I reported to him on board. He expressed great pleasure that I had returned and, particularly, that I had done so without my beard. He told me to join my squadron mates in Cairo, where they were enjoying a week's leave, and George Calder and I travelled there next day by train. I learnt that during the entire period of support for the allied invasion forces the British carrier squadrons had suffered the loss of 23 aircraft and 9 pilots. A memorable reunion ensued after our arrival in Cairo, marred only by the absence of Gerry Gowan who, on the same day that I had been shot down, was very seriously wounded and was flown ashore to hospital to have a leg amputated.

During our few days in Cairo I celebrated my 21st birthday at a fashionable open-air garden restaurant on the outskirts of the city. It was a fine party, with all the members of our squadron present but, with much regret, I suffered the next day the most abominable after-effects. We rode camels round the pyramids, swam at the Mena House Hotel, drank at Shepherds, ate countless prawn cocktails and generally made the most of our holiday. All too soon, however, it came to an end; reality returned and we were back on board at Alex. So much for the two months' home leave I had been promised at my debriefing in the headquarters ship.

On returning to the squadron I found that my Section Leader, George Ogilvy, had taken photographs of me with his oblique F24 aerial camera as I came down by parachute. He had watched my burning Seafire roll over and dive straight into the ground. On impact he had photographed the resulting column of flame and smoke. Thinking this was the funeral pyre of his long-time flying mate, he was about to set off back to the ship when he spotted my parachute. He then took two shots of me in the air, and one more just after landing, with me on the ground struggling to gather in the partially collapsed canopy. I know of no other airman who has such a record of himself coming down behind enemy lines. I think these superbly clear photos may be unique and they fill a special place in my album.

I learnt that George Ogilvy, after watching my safe arrival on terra firma, had flown back to the fleet but, being short of fuel, he landed on another, nearer, carrier to replenish. Thus it was that, of the four of us who had taken off on the dawn sortie, only one, George Calder's wing-man, returned to *Attacker* at the scheduled time. This was a poor start to our first day back on operations after the break at Maddalena but, of course, the gloom was somewhat lightened when Ogilvy arrived back on board later that morning.

*Chapter 6*

# Back to Sea (1944)

*The Isles of Greece, the Isles of Greece...*
*Where grew the arts of war and peace* – Lord Byron

In the next two months HMS *Attacker*, with three other carriers, made several sorties from Alexandria to the Aegean. Enemy positions on the islands were attacked with a view to hastening the withdrawal of the Germans from the area. Harbours and shipping particularly were targeted. My participation was mostly confined to general air patrols and fleet cover, and my last operational sortie was an hour-long photographic reconnaissance of the island of Rhodes. The anti-aircraft fire which followed us wherever we went concerned me greatly as I did not know how I could face the prospect of being shot down and again taken prisoner. All was well, however, and together with 'Nobby' Clarke, who accompanied me, I returned undamaged to our ship.

Spells of operations lasted usually for five or six days, with each pilot making two sorties per day. During these periods drinking at the bar was generally frowned upon, although perhaps a pint of beer at the end of the day was acceptable. However, once the ship had departed from the danger zone the pilots could look forward to a few days' respite from the tensions of flying over enemy territory. It was then that the wardroom piano came into its own, masterfully played by our very own squadron pianist Walter 'Butch' Buchan, a doughty Scot. He played entirely by ear and, as long as a repetitive supply of liquor was placed before him, he became the centrepiece of a lengthy night of noisy relaxation.

One day we anchored off the island of Chios. Our arrival closely followed the departure of the German garrison and we were the first warship to appear. Our reception was overwhelming, as flower-laden boatloads of islanders approached and clustered round our ship. This unexpected and emotional welcome touched our hearts.

It was only when we went ashore that we understood the depth of their joy at Liberation. The children, and there were many of them, all had spindly legs and pot bellies. They had been deprived of milk and the foods needed for their proper development and it was obvious that their sufferings under German occupation had been harsh in the extreme.

We stayed for a few days at this lovely island set in the clear waters of the sunlit Aegean Sea. Each time we went ashore we took loaves of bread, tins of cheese, chocolate and any other treats available from our ship's canteen. Every house had an open door and a welcome, often made memorable by children playing mandolins to accompany their traditional Greek folksongs – so charming, moving and never-to-be-forgotten.

We sailed away feeling humbled by what we had encountered. Later, as the first ship to call at the island of Mytilene, we experienced the same welcome and the same evidence of cruel deprivation by the enemy.

From time to time during my tour of duty in No. 879 squadron, HMS *Attacker*, with other vessels of the fleet, spent short periods in harbour. On those occasions, in places such as Gibraltar, Malta, Algiers or Alexandria, it was rarely possible for every ship to be given a berth alongside a jetty. So it was not unusual at these times for a British submarine to be secured to the side of our carrier, giving us the opportunity to exchange social visits with our brethren who fought the war in perilous circumstances beneath the surface of the oceans, in contrast to us who operated in the skies above it. We soon discovered a bond of good fellowship between submariners and aviators, born, I believe, from the awareness that we each worked in an environment unfamiliar and probably unknown to our naval colleagues who fought their battles on the surface.

The way of life, the personal feelings and experiences of men serving in a submarine in wartime were known only to submariners. In the same way aviators were alone in their understanding and experience of fighting the war in the air. It was always a pleasure to enjoy for a few days the more than lively company of the submarine crews. Certainly we regarded them with the greatest admiration.

## Chapter 7

# Batsman (1945–6)

In due course I received from the Irvin Air Chute Company the golden caterpillar brooch signifying that my life had been saved by the use of one of their parachutes. With this charming and much-coveted emblem I became an official member of the famous Caterpillar Club.

Between each of our three sorties to the Aegean we spent a few days in Alexandria. The bar of the Cecil Hotel was always our shore-side rendezvous where, not infrequently accompanied by our admirable and supportive Padre, the Rev. Basil Watson, we were entranced by the 'gully-gully' men, the conjurors who produced live fluffy chicks from empty space, from everywhere and nowhere.

Most evenings began with glasses of Stella beer at the Cecil, to be followed by a meal at one of Alex's fine eating places. Thereafter the city offered endless choices for a night out, to be concluded with a hilarious ride in an open carriage, a gharri, as we returned to our ship.

In the splendid harbour of Alex my friend George Calder and I taught ourselves to sail. We soon mastered the techniques of managing the local craft, the felucca, with a single lateen sail. Thus was initiated my enduring love of sailing.

The small carriers from which we operated were not capable of the high speeds which the big carriers could achieve. Our maximum speed with a clean hull was 18 knots but after weeks at sea our top speed was usually 16–17 knots. This meant that landing back on board was often a hazardous operation, especially when the ocean swell caused up-and-down movement of the deck. The state of the ocean, the strength of the wind, the pitch of the deck and the small size of our carriers were often of greater concern to us than the danger from the main enemy on land or under the sea.

Within the squadron a close comradeship existed between the pilots, and between them and the skilled fitters, riggers and armourers who maintained our aircraft, together with those who packed our parachutes. These men, who worked endless hours by day and by night to keep our aircraft serviceable, justified completely the absolute faith we had in them. Except when I suffered damage from enemy fire, I never had a serious failure in flight.

I remember all my squadron mates of those days with great affection. Amongst our number, as was general in all Fleet Air Arm squadrons, were several New Zealanders. They claimed that they came from the most beautiful country in the world. I wanted to believe them, even though I came from British Columbia, but I could not help wondering how, if their homeland was so wonderful, they could bear to leave it to travel thousands of miles over U-boat-ridden oceans to take part in a European war. How could they choose to be bombed in London, bombed in Portsmouth and, furthermore, to join one of the most hazardous branches of the armed services and fly aircraft from tiny carriers on dangerous and stormy seas? It struck me that these men from 'Down-Under' must be seekers after a challenge and that, when they found one, they were driven to meet it.

Well, thank God they were, for they came in great numbers to Britain in the 1940s to form a significant proportion of aircrew in our naval squadrons.

I first came into contact with the New Zealanders whilst on my flying training course. They made a lively group comprising strong and distinctive personalities. If there were any insignificant Kiwis, I never met one in the Fleet Air Arm. My association with them was established when, with two other British students, I was co-opted into their Haaka war-dance team to make up numbers. We learnt three Haakas and put on a show on several occasions in Canada, in a probably vain attempt to terrify the audience. When we returned to the UK, I reaped my reward by enjoying the occasional slice of rich fruit cake which loving families in New Zealand sent to their sons serving overseas.

When, after long months at sea, or ashore in Africa or Italy, we returned to the UK for a break, these Kiwis regarded it, as we did, as 'coming home'. Such was the amazing loyalty of these men from the other side of the world. I wonder if we realised at the time how fortunate we were to have these stalwart characters alongside us. Sadly, a considerable number of the hundreds who served never returned to their homeland, and were never to know the freedom and peace enjoyed by those of us who survived.

One of my closest friends was a New Zealander, Sub Lieutenant Harris. He came several times to my home and was much liked by my family. It seems hard to believe now that I knew him only by his nickname 'Shorty', and that I never learnt his address or knew even whether he came from North Island or South Island. When our training came to an end we went our separate ways and to this day I do not know whether he survived the war. Such was life in the services in those days. We came together, stayed awhile and then moved on in a fast and ever-changing world. How I regret now that I did not keep in touch with so many erstwhile friends.

The affection in which I hold these courageous wartime friends was reinforced in 1998 when my wife and I visited their country. We received the most heart-warming welcome and hospitality from old shipmates, particularly Jim Howden, Neil Ganley and Gordon Reece, the last two of whom I had not seen since the end of 1944. Even though a few more wrinkles were evident, they were the same lively, warm-hearted friends I had lived and flown with all those years ago. We travelled extensively on this memorable tour. Above all we can confirm the sentiment expressed by my old squadron mates from New Zealand – yes, this is the most beautiful country in the world.


After returning to the UK I left 879 Squadron and was granted two weeks' leave. I headed for Barrington to spend it with my parents. On the sixth day of my leave I received a phone call from my appointments officer at Admiralty in Whitehall instructing me to report forthwith to Easthaven in Scotland to undertake a Deck Landing Control Officers (DLCO) Course. Picturing him sitting in his comfortable chair in his warm, plush office at Queen Anne's Mansions, I remonstrated with him, explaining that I had been promised 14 days' leave, not to mention the two months promised earlier after my escape from captivity. He refused to reconsider the timing of my new appointment and when, again, I expressed my dissatisfaction his sharp comment was, 'There is a war on, you know.' That remark has always stuck in my mind. I departed for Scotland the following day.

The DLCO's, or Batsman's, role in deck landing was to assist the approaching pilot to make his arrival at the right speed and at the right place. The escort carriers were tiny and the landing area, in which an arrester wire could be 'caught' by the tail hook, was minimal. With the ship pitching up and down, a fine judgement was required. The course at Easthaven was designed to teach us the techniques and to ensure our competence in a responsible job.

Whilst on the course I received a congratulatory telegram from my parents. This was my first intimation that I had been awarded an MBE (Military). They had seen it published in the *Daily Telegraph* extract from the *London Gazette*, where the citation was for 'gallantry and devotion to duty'. I regarded this at the time as a great honour and I, together with my old friend Peter 'Sheepy' Lamb, who was on the course with me, seized the first opportunity to take the train to Edinburgh for a night of celebration – mostly in Rose Street, now a string of little boutique shops but then composed almost entirely of pubs. This was a memorable night out and when next day we returned to Easthaven nursing sore heads, we knew once more that recurrent 'never again' feeling.

Throughout our training as DLCOs we were favoured by the services of a team of navy pilots whose whole purpose in life was to fly endless circuits of the airfield, so that the pupil batsmen could practise controlling them on their approaches to imaginary deck landings. After each touch-down they opened up and went round again for another circuit. They continued going round and round until shortage of fuel gave them reason to take a break from this giddy procedure. They were known as 'clockwork mice'. Whether these pilots found this process enjoyable or whether they were doing it as a punishment for some past misdemeanour we never knew, but they did a job for us that, clearly, had to be done by someone.

To gain the experience needed by the students several different types of aircraft were employed by the clockwork mice. Each type presented its own unique problems to the pilot, especially the restriction of his view ahead on the approach to a landing. On many types this was seriously obscured by a long, broad nose ahead of the cockpit. Each type had its own particular attitude on the approach and its own characteristics on landing. An understanding of all these special factors was fundamental to the work of the DLCO.

On completion of the course I was appointed as DLCO and Flight Deck Officer to HMS *Chaser*, an escort carrier about to sail for the Far East as part of the British Pacific Fleet. No. 899 Squadron was the resident Seafire squadron on board. This was the squadron in which I had served for the Salerno landings in 1943 and several of my old friends were still there. Once again back at Long Kesh in Northern Ireland, I joined the squadron there for an intensive spell of dummy deck landings on the airfield, getting to know all the pilots and working to build mutual confidence, an essential element in the relationship between pilots and batsman.

At the same time, when free evenings allowed, we renewed former acquaintance with the Officers' Club in Belfast, that best of all spots for serious relaxation in the company of allies from many nations.

After Christmas and a short work-up in the Clyde estuary, we left home waters and set off for Australia, via the Mediterranean and the Suez Canal. We were on our way before I could be called to an investiture at the Palace to receive my MBE. I expected that, if I survived the war against the Japanese, I would enjoy the honour of an investiture when I returned home. Sadly, by the time I did so some two years later, the King, perhaps due to poor health, had ceased presenting medals to recipients of such lowly orders as the MBE.


On our arrival in Sydney we came under the command of the C-in-C British Pacific Fleet, Admiral Sir Bruce Fraser. Our role, however, was to be part of the 'Fleet Train' and 899 Squadron was transferred to HMS *Indefatigable*, one of our big fleet aircraft carriers. From then until the end of the war in the Pacific we spent months and months at sea transporting new aircraft to the Fleet and receiving from them 'flying duds' – aircraft which could be flown to us, but which were not fit for further operational use due to war damage, or which needed major overhaul. After landing aboard, the flying duds were struck down into our hangar and brand new planes were ranged on deck to be flown off to replenish the first-line squadrons.

The beautiful city of Sydney was our rear base. We returned there about every three months for a short break. From there to our forward base at Manus, one of the Admiralty Islands between New Guinea and New Britain, was a five-day voyage. From Manus to the Fleet operating areas off the islands still occupied by Japan was another five-day trip. When we had delivered all our new aircraft to the big carriers and had acquired a full load of 'duds', we returned to Manus to replenish with new aircraft and stores, before repeating the operation again and again.

Manus would nowadays be described as a tropical paradise of palm trees, golden sands, and clear lagoons swarming with exotic fish and shells. I'm afraid that at the time we regarded it in a different light and longed to be back in Britain with our families or, at least, in the wonderful city of Sydney, where we had already made good friends amongst the incredibly generous people of that city.

We had our own landing strip on the atoll of Manus and, when ashore, we lived in tents or native huts in the shade of the palm trees. The flying foxes roosted above us until, with a great flapping, they took off en masse each evening on their foraging expeditions. At low tide the warm water of the lagoon became a wonderland of rippling colour. Wearing stout footwear and carrying a sturdy stick, it was possible to wade safely out to the reef, taking care not to step into a giant clam with its powerful wide-open jaws, or on to one of the countless spiny sea urchins. The clear water abounded in fish and coral painted in brilliant rainbow hues. On the reef itself striped sea snakes of fearsome appearance slithered at high speed across the coral. We searched especially for a spiral shell with a trap-door attached to the snout of the fish inside. This door was patterned with an attractive eye-like marking. We knew them as 'cat's-eyes'. The fit of the door in the mouth of the shell was so perfect that, even with the point of a sharp knife, it could not be dislodged. The answer was to bury the shells in the sand by our tent, where the fish would be eaten by ants overnight and the cat's-eyes released. We treasured them and, after polishing, they became things of glossy beauty.


Victory in Europe was declared one day when we were in the sweltering heat of Leyte Gulf in the Philippines. We had more than a few drinks in celebration but felt even more isolated out in the Far East. The Japanese were an implacable enemy who defended to the death and we could see no prospect of the war ending for at least another two years, if then.

All the large British carriers suffered from kamikaze attacks, with some appalling consequences. We in the Fleet Train were most fortunate to escape these fearsome onslaughts, but conditions on board for such long periods at sea were unpleasant indeed. The climate was tropical and the weather was invariably hot. With no air conditioning, the inside of the ship became an oven which barely cooled, even at night. Everyone suffered from skin diseases such as ringworm, infected prickly heat, and rashes of mysterious kinds caused by excessive and continuous sweating. We greatly missed fresh food and vegetables, which were unknown after the first few days at sea. There was one feature in our lives, however, with which we had no cause for complaint, that was the regular delivery of mail from home. The Fleet Post Office system was remarkably efficient. They employed every possible means to get letters, newspapers and packages to us with no delay. It was quite astonishing to receive a sudden delivery of mail by ship or by air, when we were at sea in the midst of the vast Pacific Ocean, and to find that the letters had been written in Britain only four or five days previously. The arrival of mail was a salient event in our lives, even if men sometimes received news which they did not wish to hear.

With no prospect in sight of the war ending, we were astonished at the news of the dropping of the atomic bombs on Hiroshima and Nagasaki. When, a few days later, we learnt of the surrender of Japan, our joy was unbounded. At first we were hesitant to believe the news reports – they just seemed too good to be true – but when it was confirmed, slowly we became convinced that, at last, the long war was over. For most of us the six years of war had dominated our young lives so completely that we could scarcely imagine how we were to adjust to an unfamiliar, non-violent, world of peace. But whatever our uncertainties, we could hardly wait to get ashore and taste the fruits of freedom.

Our impatient wait was not a long one, for in no time at all we, with many units of the British Pacific Fleet, entered the magnificent harbour of Hong Kong amidst scenes of wild celebration. We stayed there for several days to receive the formal surrender of the Japanese forces in this British colony. After only a few hours, with the renowned resilience of the Chinese, their little jobbing tailors were again in business. One of them was on board our ship almost as soon as we had dropped anchor and, with peacetime dinners in the wardroom again in prospect, I got myself measured for a white mess jacket. I was able to supply the tailor with the necessary white 'duck' material, which I bought from the ship's store. The following morning my jacket was delivered – a perfect fit and needing no adjustment.

Apart from the great assembly of British Pacific Fleet warships, the anchorage was alive with junks and sampans criss-crossing the sunlit harbour as they engaged in their daily business. They, too, were celebrating a long-awaited liberation from a hated enemy who had suppressed them cruelly and who, with their heartless brutality, had caused such widespread suffering. Electricity generating stations in the colony had been destroyed but, when darkness fell, celebrations erupted, with rockets, flares and fireworks of all kinds filling the night sky, lighting up Hong Kong's spectacular harbour and its steep hilly backdrop.

Leaving behind parties of engineers to help with the restoration of essential services in the colony, we sailed from Hong Kong for our six-day voyage to Australia, and for our long-awaited return to the wonderfully kind and generous friends that we had made in Sydney on earlier visits.

## Chapter 8

# Peace at Last (1945)

Back in Australia, all aircrew disembarked from the carriers, which were thenceforth to be used for transporting numbers of former Japanese prisoners of war and internees from places all over the Pacific. Because the means of getting us home to Britain were so limited, thousands of us were given total freedom to live where we wished in Sydney. One of my shipmates, Ken Rich, and I rented a flat near King's Cross from where we could easily get into the centre of Sydney by tram. Walking from our flat to the tram stop, we passed a row of shops, one of which was a milk bar. On board ship, after the first few days at sea, all needs for milk were provided by the powdered variety. We were assured that it gave the same nutritional value that fresh milk offered, but it had an unattractive appearance and an unappetising flavour. Naturally, over many months we grew accustomed to it and accepted it as if it were normal but, when we came ashore, the chance to drink the real thing was irresistible. Ken and I made an agreement that we would never walk past the milk bar. On every trip betwixt tram stop and flat we would go in and sink a pint of this most delectable, ice-cold, full-cream liquor. In the evenings the bar of the Australia Hotel was the most favoured rendezvous for many disembarked, freedom-loving Fleet Air Arm aviators, but in those days all bars had, by law, to close at six o'clock. Quick drinking was therefore the order of the day. Later, after a meal, the popular spots were Prince's or Romano's, where, with the girlfriends that most of us had by then acquired, we danced the night away.

On previous visits to the city I, like many others, had made good Australian friends. Dr and Mrs Byron Ruse from the lovely North Shore suburb of Wahroonga had been most kind to me in the past, and after I had been ashore for a few weeks they invited me to stay at their home. They had a son, Bill, and an attractive daughter, Margaret. From the age of 17 until now, aged 22, I had been constantly on the move and was never in any one place for more than a few days or, at most, a few weeks, except when at sea in a ship. This opportunity to enjoy the carefree life, which is taken for granted by youngsters these days, was unknown to me and to most of my colleagues. We made the most of our chances and my five months ashore in Sydney was the most memorable time of my life. It happened to coincide with the height of the summer, from September to February. The Ruses owned a holiday cottage at Newport Beach and we stayed there over Christmas and New Year. Sydney, with its night life, its incomparable harbour, its glorious sandy surfing beaches and its friendly people was a wonderland to us.

With the war over at last, a joyous atmosphere of freedom and good-fellowship reigned throughout and, with so many hundreds of Fleet Air Arm aircrew enjoying it, we seemed to have taken the city over completely. It could not last for ever, though, and it was with a leaden heart that I received directions to take passage home in the liner *Athlone Castle*. I shall remember for ever my friends in Sydney and the happy times they gave me. I kept in touch with the Ruses until they died and I hope that I was able to convey to them the huge gratitude that I felt for their amazing kindness to me.


One day in December whilst in Sydney I had been astonished to receive an envelope with an Arizona, USA, postmark. It was addressed to me at my parents' home in England and had been forwarded. Inside was a letter from an American farmworker. He told me that he had two German prisoners of war, Konrad and Kurt, working with him. They had given him my address and he had decided to let me know about them. I was naturally thrilled to receive this news and I replied at once, enclosing Christmas cards for my two former conspirators. Having re-established contact with them in this almost unbelievable way, I have kept in touch with them ever since by letters and cards, and by visits to them at their homes. They too have visited me in Britain.

It transpired that they were moved from France to a prison camp in Morocco, near Casablanca. After some time there they were shipped to a cotton-picking plantation in Arizona. They were there for two years and learnt to speak quite good American. Then followed a period at a camp in Yorkshire before they were repatriated to their homes in 1948. Konrad told me that in Grignan he had reported to an SS unit, informing them that he had a British prisoner who was to be handed over to the proper authority. The SS officer refused to accept me and Konrad was ordered to take me to an isolated place and put a bullet through me. Hitler's personal order in the spring of 1944 that escaping airmen were to be shot was, presumably, behind this, but the instruction confirmed Konrad in his wish to join forces with me. And so it was that my run of good fortune was initiated. Many years later, on an occasion when Konrad and his family were staying at my home, I invited my old friend George Ogilvy to join us for lunch. He had watched me parachuting into enemy territory and into almost immediate captivity, so he was interested to meet one of the German soldiers who had held me prisoner. Konrad's mastery of the English language, after several years in the USA, was better than our knowledge of German and a lively discussion ensued as we reviewed the events we had experienced those many years ago. During the meal, while comradeship and good fellowship reigned, I took this perfect opportunity to raise a glass to Konrad across the table and thank him, with great sincerity, for not shooting me!


On my way home from Australia in the *Athlone Castle* we called at Bombay for several days. My brother Barry, who had been released from the Navy some months earlier, was back in his pre-war job there with the wine merchants Cutler Palmer. He took me under his wing, put me up in his house and showed me something of the good life he enjoyed. The sporting clubs with their superb facilities were an eye-opener to me and I felt more than a little envious of his way of life.

Soon after arriving home I was called to a Demobilisation Centre near Manchester. There, on 30th April 1946, I received my discharge from the Royal Navy. It was just over five years since I had joined. As a token of our nation's gratitude for services rendered I was presented with a civilian suit, a trilby hat, a tie, a pair of shoes and a raincoat. With that my pay was stopped. In common with several million other demobbed servicemen I emerged from the centre a free man to face an unfamiliar world. Like many of my fellows I had returned home from a war on the other side of the globe with no career mapped out and no firm plans for new employment. To make a future was the next big adventure.

# Chapter 9

# *Civilian (1946–7)*

*And bade his messengers ride forth,*
*East and west and south and north* – Macaulay

Once out of the Navy I began the search for a permanent job. In London one day I called at the Foreign Office to see if there were any openings there. Having no appointment to meet anyone I was unable to get past the doorkeeper. He was a friendly chap and, whilst I talked to him, a black official car drew up. The passenger who emerged from it entered the building with a cheery greeting to the doorman, who explained to me that he was a King's Messenger. When I asked how one became such a person, he replied that they were ex-officers but were all much older than me. After further discussion, although he would not allow me into the office, he said he would get me a form for applying for a position in the Foreign Office. When I took this home I decided to fill it in and, in the section asking which department I wished to join, I wrote 'King's Messenger'. I mailed it off, but only as a sort of lark, and I was not surprised when I received no acknowledgement. I soon forgot the matter.

I was attracted to the idea of becoming a surveyor. I imagined it to be a healthy outdoor life and I was accepted for a place at a college in Southampton, to start a course in the summer. Then one morning several weeks later I received a letter from the Foreign Office inviting me to attend an interview for the appointment as a King's Messenger. I was astonished at this and, as I travelled to London, I felt I must be wasting everyone's time. However, the interview was not too frightening and only a few days passed before I was asked to undergo a medical exam and to attend a further

81

interview. At this more details of the job were explained to me and I was formally offered a post. One point was emphasised – this was that if any document was lost, no excuse whatever would be accepted, even if there were special extenuating circumstances. Instant dismissal without appeal would result.

To accept this post meant forgoing my surveyor's course and I had a lengthy discussion with my father as to what would be best for me. In words which I remember exactly, he said, 'I know what you ought to do – but I know what I would do.' That settled it and my college course was cancelled. In a matter of days I was on my way to Hong Kong to start a 12-month tour of duty based at this fascinating and exciting colonial outpost.

In these days of rapid worldwide travel it seems incredible that my journey from London Northolt to Hong Kong took me nine days. Armed with my treasured 'silver greyhound' insignia and my special diplomatic passport, I set off by BOAC in an Avro York airliner, a post-war development of the Lancaster bomber. We made night stops at Cairo, Karachi and Calcutta where, because there was no onward flight available, I stayed for four days at the Great Eastern Hotel. Coming from the austere conditions in Britain I found the amenities and food at this fine hotel quite wondrous. The great panelled dining room with the minstrel's gallery, the glistening chandeliers and the ranks of punkahs turning silently above, was the setting for tables laid with crisp white cloths and gleaming tableware. The staff in their immaculate white uniforms with scarlet sashes and headwear made a sparkling and, for me, an exotic scene. After this, my first taste of the exciting and mysterious East, I was able to proceed to Hong Kong by RAF Transport Command Dakota. This trip took a further three days, staying overnight at Rangoon, Bangkok and Saigon. The York and the Dakota were not pressurised and, like other piston-engined aircraft of their day, were extremely noisy so that, after several days in the air, the passengers were fatigued, partially deaf and jangling all over from the constant vibration.

Many of the King's Messengers who in pre-war days had been accustomed to making long and leisurely journeys by ship and train had continued to serve long after their normal retiring age. They went on with their travelling for the duration of the war, often in difficult and dangerous conditions. For example, to convey documents to Sweden they flew in the bomb bay of a Mosquito fighter-bomber.

This must have been a freezing and most uncomfortable experience, especially for elderly men.

At the end of the war many of these long-serving gentlemen left the Service and the Foreign Office decided to employ some younger KMs more fitted to cope with the strenuous conditions of post-war travel. Scheduled flights were few and far between and the aircraft used were often wartime military planes unsuited to comfortable travel. Nevertheless, flying for business was becoming the norm and the days of leisurely voyages by ship were over. Three younger men were taken on and, at the age of 22, I was the youngest King's Messenger that had ever been appointed.


Classified mail was brought from London and delivered to our office in Hong Kong. I was one of five KMs based there, accommodated in considerable comfort at the Peninsula Hotel in Kowloon. Our job was to convey mail to British embassies and consulates throughout the Far East, from Calcutta in the west, Tokyo and Manila in the east, Manchuria in the north, and throughout mainland China from Peking in the north to Kunming, close to the borders of Tibet and Burma. I was fascinated by this vast and exciting country where countless millions of people lived in great poverty but seemed always to be laughing, smiling and joking. They introduced me to the world's most interesting and delicious food.

The Peninsula was at that time the finest hotel in the colony. Today ultra-modern luxury hotels abound on Hong Kong island and on the mainland in Kowloon, but the famous Peninsula still holds its own for elegance, comfort and traditional service. When I had paid my first visit to Hong Kong in HMS *Chaser* at the end of the Pacific war, the colony was in a state of devastation following the Japanese occupation and surrender. Now, only nine months later, the British administration, with the incomparable enthusiasm and dedication to hard work of the Hong Kong Chinese, had restored all the public services to working order. Everything functioned at full efficiency: electricity supplies, water supplies, telephones, road and water transport, including the celebrated Star Ferries which ran continuously by day and by night from Victoria on Hong Kong island to Kowloon on the mainland. The amazing spirit of enterprise which characterised the Chinese was evident in the shops of the town. They were bulging with goods from all over the world. Quality clothing materials, watches and jewellery, fine china and foodstuffs were all readily available and at rock-bottom prices. It was an eye-opener to me as in Britain none of these things was obtainable by an ordinary citizen. Restaurants and small eating places abounded and, in the evenings, the clatter of mah-jong tiles resounded along the pavements as locals played their favourite game. The whole colony was, after less than a year of peace, already humming with activity and enterprise. To anyone coming from a dreary post-war Britain the atmosphere of 'can-do' enthusiasm was uplifting and infectious.

Enjoying meals in small Chinese eating-places soon became a feature of my life in Hong Kong. I had never before experienced the exciting flavours and the wide variety of Eastern food, and I quickly developed an appetite for it which has remained with me to this day. The Peninsula Hotel had a balcony restaurant where, from time to time, I chose to eat in elegant style. The balcony overlooked the harbour, with the Peak of Hong Kong island in the background across the water. What a view it was at night! The city opposite was ablaze with lights reaching up to the summit of the Peak. Their reflections glimmered and danced on the dark water, which was alive with boats of all kinds, Star Ferries, sampans, junks, the occasional ocean-going vessel, all gliding silently across the scene. This was a romantic setting for a fine dinner on a warm summer evening.

The programme for the delivery visits which the five King's Messengers made throughout the Far East was planned by our agent. He made all our travel arrangements and assembled the bags of mail which were to be carried. We established several routes round our territory which, after trial and error, became standard. Some of these journeys involved long trips lasting many days or, occasionally, several weeks when transport aircraft became unreliable.

Completing a circuit of mainland China was one of our regular commitments. As a rule, the first leg from Hong Kong to Shanghai was flown in a military Dakota of Royal Air Force Transport Command. The Consul-General at Shanghai gave us accommodation for a couple of days before we journeyed on, often by overnight train, to Nanking, a one-time capital of China. That leg of the trip was always a particular pleasure to me as the compartments in the railway sleeping cars were beautifully appointed, superbly panelled

My father (George Edward)
with my sister Ann and a
fine Kokanee salmon at
Riondel in 1929.

My mother, Margaret Alice,
(née Webb) at Saanich,
Vancouver Island, 1916.

Initial training, HMS *St.Vincent*, January 1942. Author is extreme right, middle row.

Primary trainer - the fully aerobatic N3N3 - at USNAS Grosse Ile.

My first Spitfire.

879 Squadron Seafire L-111 at RNAS Machrihanish, 1943.

HMS *Attacker*, 1943.

With George Ogilvy - relaxing in the shade at Chrea, Algeria.

My Seafire LR 691 approaching the invasion coast, 15 August, 1944.

The funeral pyre of LR691, 21 August 1944. The long shadow cast by the flame and smoke can be seen.

Three stages in my parachute descent, 21st August 1944

Floating down

Getting close now

Safe landing - parachute collapsing.          Photographs by George Ogilvy

The hill town of Grignan - topped by the chateau, German headquarters.

Mme Madeleine Tailland at Grignan.
A gallant lady.

On leave in Cairo. A tour of the pyramids - my favourite squadron photograph.

879 squadron, HMS *Attacker* 1944.

HMS *Chaser*.

HMS *Chaser* in Hong Kong harbour on VJ Day, celebrating the Japanese surrender.

Civilian. In my 'demob suit', May 1946.

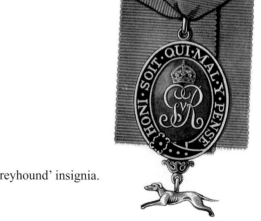

The 'silver greyhound' insignia.

Return to flying - a late variant of the Seafire.

813 Squadron - mock torpedo attack on HMS *Indomitable*.

My first supersonic flight in the US Navy FJ-3 Fury. VX-3 Squadron.

In the cockpit of a Sea Vixen at RNAS Abbotsinch, 1958.

Arriving for trials aboard HMS *Ashanti*. The ill-fated XN 334 prototype P531.

HMS *Hermes*.

On the ferry for France. Sally with the boys as we head off on holiday in 1963.

The family with Madeleine at Montélimar.

Departing Liverpool for West Africa, 1968. Sally aboard the Elder Dempster liner S.S. *Apapa*

Dressed for Remembrance Day in Freetown, 1971.

Farewell to a long career.

Lifelong friendship. With Madeleine at Montélimar, 1997.

in fine woods and offering unmatched comfort. It came as a surprise to me to find such high-quality amenities in a country so recently torn by war. Nanking was still recovering from the brutal occupation by the Japanese, which had begun in 1937 when the invading troops arrived in the region. The hideous massacre which followed, known as the 'Rape of Nanking', was still remembered by all. The torture and subsequent slaughter of over 300,000 Chinese civilian men, women and children had cast a dark shadow over the city. It still lingers to this day. Nanking, with its famous university, lies on the mighty Yangtze river, which flows for 3,500 miles throughout China, from its source high in the mountains of Tibet to Shanghai where, finally, it empties into the East China Sea. On its majestic journey it winds serenely through vast areas of rice fields and general agricultural land, cascades over gigantic waterfalls and rages through spectacular gorges. Only in superlatives could this river be described.

After a couple of days at Nanking our journey resumed by air, thenceforth with the Chinese National Aviation Corporation (CNAC), sometimes by Douglas Dakota but more often by Curtis Commando aircraft. In each case the passengers sat facing each other in two rows of canvas bucket seats which ran the length of the aircraft on each side of the cabin. They were designed for carrying fully equipped soldiers or paratroops and were still in their wartime configuration. Our next stopover was made at Hankow, now named Wuhan, some 600 miles upstream from the mouth of the Yangtze at Shanghai. Hankow was then a largely industrial town at the limit of navigability for ocean-going ships. Here, as at all our stops, the King's Messenger was met on arrival at the airport by a car from the British Mission and taken to their office to hand over the mail he had brought, and obtain a receipt for its safe delivery. Thereafter he was given accommodation, a friendly welcome and, invariably, generous hospitality by the staff, who were always eager to hear news of the outside world and of their friends at other remote posts in the Far East. Our journey then progressed, again by CNAC, to Chungking, a big city on the Yangtze a further 450 miles upstream. It lies in the foothills of the great range of mountains stretching eastwards across much of China from Tibet, and the town is built on rocky outcrops rising abruptly from the river, with steeply ascending terraced steps on all sides. Again, the British staff gave their typically warm-hearted reception, accompanying it with food and drink in plenty.

The last leg of the outward journey round China was a flight over spectacular and fearsome-looking mountains to Kunming, the capital of Yunnan province, which is bordered by Burma, Laos and Vietnam. At an elevation of 6,500 feet its climate was delightful, never being too hot. With wondrous views of lakes and mountains, it was one of my favourite stop-overs in China. The welcome which the King's Messenger received was always proportional to the remoteness of the mission he was visiting, and a few days at the fascinating and mysterious city of Kunming was, therefore, an especially memorable experience for me. On our return journey to Hong Kong we retraced our steps and called, in reverse order, at the missions we had visited on the outbound route. The aircraft in which we travelled, sitting in our bucket seats, were unpressurised, noisy, very uncomfortable and with non-existent heating. They were crewed by experienced wartime American pilots who, with remarkable skill, coped with the primitive navigation aids which were available, and with the appalling weather conditions that so frequently prevailed, especially over the massive mountain ranges of this vast country. My confidence in them was never misplaced, though I was often extremely frightened.

The days I spent in Peking I recall as ones of busy exploration. The city, and the countryside around it were unspoiled by modern development. It was rich in historic palaces and temples, so many in fact that it was not possible for me to get round to see them all. The greatest, of course, was the Forbidden City, an astonishing assemblage of royal pavilions, beautifully proportioned temples, pagodas and dwellings with delicately curving roofs and undulating tiles, all set in paved courtyards. Every open space was embellished with striking carvings and sculptures of all sizes, and in all manner of shapes. Each one had a mysterious quality and many were grotesque, but they had been fashioned with consummate skill by a long-dead craftsman.

The streets, when I was there, were mostly narrow and many were unpaved. The almost total absence of motor vehicles allowed a constant and steady stream of rickshaws and pedicabs to flow without obstruction along the dusty thoroughfares lined with little shops and restaurants. I put up in the delightful Hotel des Wagon-Lits, perhaps one of the very few hotels in Peking which offered traditional pre-war amenities in great comfort. It had a special charm about it and recently, as I was looking through a list of

Beijing hotels in a travel magazine, I was saddened to find no mention of it. I have a distressing thought that it might have been pulled down to make way for some ultra-modern version.

The British Foreign Office staff at Peking, like their colleagues throughout China, gave me kind help and guidance during my all-too-short stays in the ancient capital. A trip to a small restaurant with a group of these friends was a highlight of each visit. It was a favourite eating-place of theirs, to which we made our way by a little fleet of rickshaws. We sat in a private room awaiting the appearance of the chef, who brought some seven or eight ducks dressed ready for roasting. From these we made our selection and then, whilst they were being cooked, we settled down in good fellowship to some glasses of our favourite Chinese tipple. We were then invited to enter the kitchen area to view the ducks being roasted over live oak fires. The sight and smell of the cooking enhanced our already eager appetites. When the birds were done to perfection they were brought to our table, the meat was then expertly carved from each duck by the chef and placed on a dish. The carcasses of the birds were then removed to be used for soup. Pieces of duck and thin stems of spring onion were rolled in a pancake before being dipped into the chosen spicy sauce, to make the most delicious mouthful this world has to offer. A small bowl of soup was served before dessert. These meals, together with the friends who accompanied me, live on in my happy memories of years gone by,

On one winter journey I travelled by train from Peking to Mukden (now called Shenyang) in Manchuria, passing the Great Wall of China en route. This amazing engineering structure which still stands after 2,000 years, stretches for more than 3,700 miles across northern China. I remember little of Mukden other than the biting cold, and the fur hat with protecting ear flaps that, for reasons of survival, I found it absolutely essential to purchase there.

During my tour of duty in the Far East I made several trips to Japan. These I found particularly enjoyable, despite the devastation of the big cities. As a rule I flew from Hong Kong to Iwakuni, an air base close to the destroyed town of Hiroshima. The flight was made in a Sunderland flying boat; I was well wrapped up in blankets as the aircraft was not heated. After a short stay in Royal Air Force accommodation at Iwakuni I travelled on for two days by train to Tokyo, passing along the Inland Sea and through the most entrancing countryside. The Japanese are true artists and their villages and towns enhanced the beauty of the landscape, something we seem rarely able to achieve in modern Britain. In the final part of the rail journey the extinct volcano of Fujiyama, with its perfectly symmetrical snow-capped summit, dominated the passing scene.

Tokyo at that time was an immense wasteland of almost total destruction following the fire-bombing attacks by Super-Fortresses in the latter stages of the war. The whole city and much of its environs had been set ablaze and only a few substantial concrete or brick structures were still standing. It seemed miraculous that the buildings comprising the splendid complex of the British Embassy remained intact. I was given accommodation in a charming house on the distant outskirts of the city. It was necessary to travel this far from the centre of town to find something habitable, and the house had been acquired by the Embassy as living quarters for some of its staff. Inside this bright and cheerful house a delicious fragrance of sandalwood prevailed, delicate screening divided the rooms, and finely woven mats lay underfoot. It must have been the much-loved home of a well-to-do Japanese family. Surrounding the house was a garden in the traditional Japanese style. To stroll round the garden in the quiet of evening was pure delight. Winding paths meandered through carefully trimmed shrubs and rockeries, bordered by gently running streams. Larger pools, alive with golden carp, were crossed by graceful bridges of elegant and enchanting design.

Japan was under strict control by the allied occupation forces and there was no opportunity for me to travel round the country. Apart from the journey by train, my only excursion outside Tokyo was to Nikko, with its ancient Shinto shrines and its world-famous three-monkeys carved statue 'Hear-no-Evil, See-no-Evil, Speak-no-Evil'. It was a focus for pilgrims and a ski resort some miles to the north of the capital. There the Embassy owned a house which was made available to the staff for recreation. A feature of the house was a traditional Japanese bathroom where a deep, tiled, rectangular pool was set into the floor. It was, in effect, the hot water tank of a boiler situated on the floor below. The bath was filled with cold water from the only tap, the furnace was set alight and, while the guests passed a pleasant hour enjoying a few glasses of saki and some seafood snacks, the water in the bath steadily heated up by convection from below. When it was bath time the bathers scrubbed themselves on the surrounding tiled area, using soap and jugs of water from the pool. Once rinsed off they tested the temperature of the water in the bath and, if it was too hot, cold was added. The guests then stepped in and there they stayed whilst the water grew hotter and hotter until, eventually, they could stand it no longer. Then, lobster pink, they climbed out and took a freezing shower in the corner. The whole procedure was an effective introduction to more glasses of saki, more seafood, and a highly enjoyable evening in pleasing company.

A journey round South-East Asia to India was one of our regular excursions. From Hong Kong we travelled to Saigon (now Ho Chi Minh City), Bangkok and Rangoon on the way to our destination at Calcutta. Because air flights were uncertain and schedules unreliable, we stopped over at each place for a day or two. This gave us the opportunity to sample the atmosphere and way of life in these strange places unfamiliar, in those days, to most people in the West. Saigon, at the southern tip of Indo-China, with its broad tree-lined boulevards, revealed its French colonial heritage. The waterways were ever busy with sampans, some loaded with farm produce for sale, some lying quietly along the shoreline. On the houseboats families were preparing delicious-smelling meals, whilst children chattered and played on all sides. The bustling markets were thronged with women, so slightly built and delicate, dressed in clothes of every colour. A day in Saigon was an entrancing experience.

Following the partition of India, the most terrible communal riots broke out between Muslims and Hindus. On one of my many trips to Calcutta the bloodletting was at its height and I was transported from Dum-Dum airport to the city in an armoured car with a military escort. The streets were lined with piles of corpses and I remained within the Great Eastern Hotel throughout my stay. News stories circulated continuously of the most appalling massacres, involving children as well as men and women. This was a tragic time in that teeming city.

\*   \*   \*

In March 1947 I completed my tour in Hong Kong and returned to London to join the group of KMs based there. We covered the cities of Europe and Scandinavia, and all of South America. Such extensive travel was, in those days, for only the very few and I knew how privileged I was to have this opportunity to see so much of the world. Many of the cities of Europe were marred by large areas of destruction from wartime bombing, or heavy artillery fire from armies on the ground, particularly the Russian forces. Even two years after the war had ended Berlin, especially, was a sea of devastation so that staying there was not a pleasurable experience. In Vienna my hotel was situated close to the famous State Opera House which, though not razed to the ground, seemed to have been reduced to a shell, and was quite unusable. A smaller auditorium was, however, intact and was able to put on a season of well-known operas. I was fortunate to be there during one of these periods and to attend three performances.

The ancient capital of Czechoslovakia had a special medieval charm and the splendour and scale of the architecture of Prague was awe-inspiring. Lying astride the great river Vitava, spanned by the massive and celebrated Charles Bridge, the city was well on the way to recovery from the after-effects of war. People there were in the mood to enjoy themselves. Restaurants were well supplied with food, drink was cheap, especially the powerful spirit slivovitz, and the night-spots were well patronised, closing their doors only when the sun came up. The Czechs clearly knew how to make the best of life and, many years later, in 1968, I was saddened to learn of the violent overthrow of their government by Russian troops and of the renewed occupation of their beautiful country by the Communists.

On my European tour of duty the only city which I visited that had not suffered from war – in fact the only one that seemed to have profited greatly from it – was Stockholm. The sort of development with which we are now so familiar in all cities was already evident there. Fine road systems with great interchanges and overpasses, modern office buildings of steel and glass, glittering shops displaying expensive clothes, furniture and goods of every kind were things beyond my ken in those early days of peace. The whole capital was spotless and shining, unlike any other city on the continent. Everything that was available anywhere in the world was available in Stockholm – but at a price. On my meagre salary I was totally out of my depth in this city, though I was mightily impressed by the cleanliness and the ultra-modernity that I saw all around me.

I was fortunate to make several trips to South America, visiting Rio de Janeiro, Montevideo, Buenos Aires and Santiago. The flights were made by British South American Airways in York aircraft, with lengthy stays at each place. To travel over the Andes mountains between Argentina and Chile it was necessary to transfer to a Lancastrian, a converted Lancaster bomber. It carried 12 passengers with no pressurisation and, for the flight at 25,000 feet, we all wore oxygen masks. The heating was largely ineffective but the spectacular scenery over the magnificent mountains just below us made any discomfort worth bearing.

During a four-day visit to Moscow at the time of the Foreign Ministers' conference there in April 1947 I was privileged to attend a gala performance of *Giselle* at the Bolshoi. The star of the show was Ulanova, the renowned prima ballerina of her time. The magnificent theatre was filled to capacity with a sparkling audience. The colour and glow of the scenery and the incomparable dancing of the beautiful Ulanova, with her warm and natural smile, made this an occasion to be remembered and treasured all my life.

At the Moscva Hotel, where many of the delegates were staying, I experienced, and enjoyed, for the first time the delights of top quality caviare, offered as a prelude to every meal, even breakfast. Unaccustomed as I was to this strongly flavoured delicacy I spread it thinly on toast as I saw many others doing but, after a day or two, I relished it by the spoonful, just like a true Muscovite.


One morning in 1947, during a spell in the UK between trips, the postman rang the doorbell of our home, handed in a registered package, and demanded my signature in receipt. On opening the parcel I found a neat box and, inside it, the insignia of my MBE. It had reached me two and three-quarter years after the award was listed in the *London Gazette*. I could but wonder whether the postman knew he was acting as stand-in for King George VI. I had been proud of this award in 1944 for gallantry at the young age of 20, but to receive it in this way was a surprise and a disappointment. I was especially sorry that my mother and father were to be denied the joy of attending the Palace to witness the award ceremony.

*   *   *

During my service as a King's Messenger the Royal Navy had been experimenting with new schemes of recruitment for the Fleet Air Arm. These had not proved successful and consideration was given to offering short-term RN commissions to those ex-RNVR aircrew who had served during the war and, at its end, had been demobilised as no longer required.

It had been my wish as a schoolboy to make a career in the Royal Navy, but wartime circumstances meant that I was required to serve on a 'hostilities-only' basis, first as a seaman rating and later as an RNVR officer. At a late stage in the war when I tried to convert to an RN commission, the Navy would not permit me to do so.

When the opportunity arose to apply for an RN commission I decided to offer my services. At my interview I made it clear that I did not wish to return to the Fleet Air Arm if I was to be employed again as a Deck Landing Control Officer. I felt that I had done my full and fair share of that as DLCO and Flight Deck Officer in HMS *Chaser* during the last year of the war in the Pacific. I was assured that I would not be reappointed in that role.

On being accepted, I wrote my resignation letter to the Foreign Office and, in late 1947, bade a sad and somewhat reluctant farewell to a band of King's Messengers, some of whom had been my stalwart friends, and to a way of life which had been exciting and full of worldwide adventure. Amongst the multitude of cities I had visited I look back on Peking as the most fascinating, Prague as the most romantic and ancient, Stockholm as the most wondrously modern, Vienna as the most cultured and Montevideo as the most charming. However much these cities may now be changed, I like to remember them as they were in those early post-war days, despite the huge damage that was then so widespread throughout Europe. The countryside of Japan I recall as the most picturesque in the world. The enjoyment of my life as a King's Messenger was due in large part to the kindly welcomes that I received at every British outpost on my routes. The friends I made were of the greatest help to me in getting about in unfamiliar, often remote, places.

## Chapter 10

# Return to the RN (1947–52)

Back in naval uniform, now with straight Lieutenant's gold rings instead of the 'Wavy Navy' stripes of the RNVR, it was time to get back to flying. This was accomplished by undergoing a refresher course at RNAS Lee-on-Solent. After a few 'dual' trips in Harvards, chiefly aerobatics and instrument flying, I found myself in the familiar cockpit of a Spitfire, to experience once again the feeling of exhilaration which that aircraft engendered. The graceful curves of its clean, purposeful lines gave me a sense of delight as I approached it on the tarmac, even before I climbed in.

On completion of my refresher flying course I awaited my first appointment. When it came it instructed me to report to the Royal Naval Air Station at Lossiemouth in Scotland to join a unit there as an instructor in the school for training Deck Landing Control Officers. When I read the details of my assignment I realised that I had broken one of the well-proven but unwritten rules of service life – never let the appointing staff know what you do not wish to do, or where you do not wish to go. If you are foolish enough to do so, as I was, you can be sure that the appointer, delighting in his controlling wisdom, or pure cussedness, will act accordingly. As it turned out, my spell at 'Lossie', with the mountains, lochs and rivers of Scotland nearby, was pleasant enough and, in any case, it was not long before I got a full flying commission again, this time to No. 780 Squadron at RNAS Culdrose in Cornwall, instructing student pilots in instrument flying, during the advanced stages of their training.

Cornwall was, in 1948, an unspoiled paradise of wonderful beaches and rugged cliffs uncluttered by tourists. With few cars on the roads, traffic jams were unknown and I came to love this beautiful part of England, particularly the Lizard peninsula – exposed, on windy days, to the full fury of the wild and fearsome Atlantic but, on quiet summer afternoons, resting in green and peaceful solitude. The springy turf of the cliff tops gave inspiration for hours of tireless walking.

Flying an aircraft on instruments alone, for example in cloud or in darkness, when there are no outside visual references, requires a special skill that needs many hours of practice to acquire. As at Pensacola (see page 16), much of this practice was gained on the ground in the Link Trainer. Pilots had to learn how to assess the information given by six or seven instruments on a special 'blind flying panel' and to understand the interaction between them. When the pilot is denied any visual reference to a natural horizon, his sense of the aircraft's attitude can be misled by other senses, chiefly those given by the balance organs in the ear. These feelings can cause him to believe that the information from the instruments is wrong. If he follows his physical feelings, and not the instruments, then disaster threatens. Pilots had to be taught to put absolute trust in their instruments, for a thorough knowledge and a good technique were essential to their survival. Autopilots, so common today, were unknown in fighter aircraft. We did our work in Airspeed Oxford twin-engined aircraft with the pupil and the instructor sitting side by side. The student was covered by a special hood so that, as he could see nothing but his instruments, he was flying 'blind'. The instructor kept an external look-out as well as advising on his pupil's technique, ready to take over control if he got into difficulties. When the time came to move on, I regretted leaving the lovely county of Cornwall but I knew that the experience of the work I had done there was to be of great value to me in my future jobs.

At Little Rissington in Gloucestershire I undertook the six-month course at the RAF Central Flying School to become a fully qualified Flying Instructor. Most of the work was done in Tiger Moth and Harvard aircraft, with students flying together, one acting as 'student' and the other as 'instructor'. To become professionally qualified we had to satisfy the examiners of our competence to teach classes in meteorology, principles of flight, engine management, instrument technology etc. At the end of the course we flew Mosquito fighter bombers, Lancaster heavy bombers and Vampire jet fighters, to broaden our experience.

On completion of the course in early 1949 I was appointed to

RNAS Gosport as a member of No. 727 Squadron, instructing students in primary flying training. This gratifying work was carried out in Tiger Moth biplanes, cold in winter, delightful in summer but always intensely interesting, and especially rewarding when one's students made it to the great occasion of first solo, as most of them did. The Naval Air Station at Gosport was a grass field well suited to elementary training. With the coastal waters of Spithead and the Isle of Wight to the south, the distinctive tower at Lee-on-Solent close at hand, and Southampton Water to the west, even the most inexperienced trainee pilot could scarcely fail to find his way back to base.

Much of our flying was over the waters of Spithead and almost every day we could look down on one of the world's great ocean liners making her way up to Southampton Water, or leaving there outward bound to an exciting destination. We were still in the age of ocean travel and these majestic and superbly comfortable vessels supplied the needs of almost all world travellers. Airlines, though well established within continents, had not yet become a serious threat to the great ocean-going ships. The sad days of their departure from the scene were still some years away. The Queens, *Mary* and *Elizabeth*, the SS *United States*, the SS *France*, the SS *America* were just a few of the imposing vessels which passed beneath us on their regular transatlantic runs. We could not deny the feelings of envy which were aroused in us as we looked down on them from 500 feet, imagining the good life being enjoyed by a thousand or more well-heeled passengers.


This highly enjoyable and most satisfying of jobs could not last for ever, though, and in the spring of 1950 I was appointed to No. 813 Squadron, equipped with Blackburn Firebrand torpedo attack aircraft. Powered by a single Bristol Centaurus engine this large single-seat tailwheel aircraft had a huge nose which, to accommodate the massive engine, extended 16 feet ahead of the cockpit. It was said that if the aircraft should inadvertently run into or fly into anything, the pilot would at least be 16 feet from the accident. However, it was a very robust machine, and when my old friend Maurice Tibby was forced to ditch in the sea because of mechanical failure, he was able to make a successful escape, to be rescued by a Royal Navy frigate. The pilot's view ahead on the landing approach was totally obscured, making the approach to a carrier landing even more difficult and hazardous than in the Seafire. Because of this, only highly experienced pilots were appointed to this squadron, with no youngsters to take the junior positions. We were attached first to HMS *Implacable* and, later, to HMS *Indomitable*, two large Fleet carriers which, together with several other carriers and the battleship HMS *Vanguard*, formed part of the, then, mighty Home Fleet.

During a spell in Gibraltar the Fleet held its annual sporting tournaments. My schoolboy success in shooting on the open ranges at Bisley prompted me to have another go at the sport, although it was over ten years since I had fired a rifle on the ranges. I put in my bid for a place in the competition. It was accepted and, for three days, I took part in the various events. After such a long period with no practice I did not expect to have much success but, with much satisfaction, I found that my shots were hitting the targets in the right places and, to my considerable surprise, I ended the contest as Home Fleet Individual Champion. To prove to myself in future years that it was not just a dream, I received an engraved shield, presented by the Commander-in-Chief.

Our flagship's home base was at Portsmouth and, when she was berthed there, the squadron flew off to our friendly shore base at the Naval Air Station, Lee-on-Solent. While there we lived comfortably in the fine wardroom mess. At Lee I shared a cabin with Dennis White, an old friend from flying training days in the USA. On his new and much prized gramophone he played recordings of Bach's Brandenburg Concertos at every opportunity. I had little choice but to listen and, over time, I came to appreciate Bach's unmistakable style. Now, half a century later, the concertos give me a special pleasure whenever I hear them, and always remind me of those agreeable days at Lee.

Throughout my two years in No. 813 Squadron we spent many months at sea in north Atlantic waters and in the Mediterranean. This was my first experience of serving at sea in a peacetime appointment, and our many 'showing the flag' visits to foreign countries made for much variety and enjoyment in our lives. We specialised in torpedo-dropping attacks and on practising the navigational skills needed to find our targets, often at long range. In the Firebrand, a single-seat aircraft, all navigation was pre-planned by the pilots before take-off. Flying aids indicating position were not available to us in those days, so that our 'dead-reckoning' calculations had to be made with great care and accuracy. To help us we employed a new grid navigation system which, with modifications designed by Lieutenant 'Smoky' Cowling, our squadron mathematical genius, proved very effective. We often went off in pairs on practice torpedo 'strikes' at the Firebrand's maximum range. Almost without exception I flew in company with my good friend, and cricket lover, John Shoebridge. After a long flight over a featureless sea I think we were always a bit surprised, as well as mightily relieved, to sight our carrier on a wide ocean at the end of our sortie.

On board ship I shared a cabin with Peter 'Bill' Brewer. We decided to learn to play chess and, each evening before dinner, we had a game. Over many months gradually we became more proficient and we felt that we were mastering the game until, one day, someone pointed out to us that we had been setting out the pieces wrongly. We had been placing the bishops where the knights should have been, and vice-versa. After that our game became hopelessly confusing, we never regained our capability, our interest waned and we went to the bar for a couple of drinks instead. Bill was a firm friend and a skilled aviator and I was greatly saddened when, a few years later, he was lost at sea in a Sea Venom night-fighter during carrier operations. In common with all squadrons, we were a close-knit group of friendly colleagues and a two-year stint at sea with this not-too-popular aircraft was no bar to future advancement. Two of our Senior Pilots, Ian Robertson and Gus Halliday, went on to hold posts of great distinction and ended their careers as Admirals.


Whilst on a Home Fleet visit to the naval base at Invergordon in north-eastern Scotland, an escape and evasion exercise was laid on to take part in wild country to the west of the base. Aircrew from all the squadrons were taken out after dark in closed lorries and deposited in pairs at different places in unknown and strange territory. The aim was to make our way undetected, and within 24 hours, to a finishing point some 25 miles away. We were opposed by police and army units whose job was to find and arrest us. Bill Brewer was my companion when we were dropped off. It did not take us long to work out where we were and, once having established our position, we knew in what direction we should make our way to our first contact point. All went well until we came to a river. Whilst crossing it we lost touch with each other in the darkness. We could not shout loudly to each other for fear of giving ourselves away to the 'enemy' and, although we spent some time trying, we failed to regain contact. Thereafter we remained separated and had to continue on our own. Probably some members of the SAS, who are expert at this sort of thing, could give an explanation for our losing each other at night in strange country, but for us it remained a mystery. I lasted out until the following afternoon, when I was captured by some soldiers. There were so many searchers in the area that to avoid them meant taking cover and that would make it impossible to reach our destination within the time limit. When the exercise ended, almost the only man from the whole air group to succeed in reaching the assigned destination was a gallant fellow pilot of No. 813 Squadron, the determined and indomitable David Crofts.

It was whilst in 813 Squadron that I joined the illustrious and unashamed group of navy pilots who have suffered the indignity of entering the 'barrier'. On my 152nd deck landing, my 83rd in the Firebrand, I floated over all the wires, drifted off to starboard, and came to an abrupt stop in a tangled web of cables. My starboard wing came off as it struck the right-hand stanchion of the barrier. The impact caused the aircraft to swing around and, in the rotation, the port wing came off as it hit the island structure. I was left in a wingless fuselage facing aft alongside the island. I raised my eyes to Commander (Air), who looked down on me from his flying control bridge. He did not appear to be pleased.

However by taking every opportunity to keep watch on the bridge as Assistant Officer-of-the-Watch, I was able to take and pass my exams for full qualification and, in due course, I was presented with my Sea Watchkeeping Certificate by Captain Manley Power, our Flag Captain. Thereafter, when flying operations allowed, I stood watch by day and by night, in charge of the mighty *Indomitable*.

During a spell in the UK in 1950 I met Sally. She was a friend of my sister Ann and was staying at Knockwood when I came up from Lee-on-Solent to spend a weekend at home with my parents. By the time I had to return to my squadron two days later, I had decided that I must somehow see more of this pretty and very personable girl. Her home was at Rowledge near Farnham in Surrey, and whilst my ship was in home waters I took every opportunity to visit her there. Her father, George Philip, a retired naval Captain with a specialist Gunnery Officer background, had commanded two aircraft carriers, HMS *Argus* and HMS *Furious*, during the war. He therefore had a particular interest in the Fleet Air Arm and a special knowledge of its value, having participated in the fearsome and long-drawn-out battles of the Malta convoys, and having launched his aircrews on sorties to attack the great German battleship *Tirpitz* in Norwegian waters. It was my good fortune that he and his wife Milly gave me a kindly welcome. As my friendship with Sally blossomed, we became engaged at New Year 1951 and, well escorted by my best man, Tom Innes, and a number of my squadron mates, we were married on 6th October 1951, in the lovely village church at Rowledge.

No sooner was our short honeymoon over than, back on board *Indomitable*, we sailed for another two months of exercises in the Mediterranean with some short but enjoyable calls at Gibraltar and Malta. By the end of 1951 my two-year spell at sea with No. 813 Squadron was completed and, once more based at home, Sally and I began our married life together.

My next appointment was to the Empire Test Pilots School at the Royal Aircraft Establishment, Farnborough. This was a one-year course comprising much 'back-to-school' classroom work, countless hours analysing the results of flights made in the aircraft of the school fleet, and writing reports. Many were the midnight hours spent poring over pages of figures obtained from a flight which had lasted, perhaps, for only an hour or so. The ETPS aircraft covered a full range of types, the largest of which were four-engined Lincoln heavy bombers, the smallest little Chipmunk trainers. In between were Viking/Valetta transports, Meteor jet and Sea Fury piston-engined fighters and a number of others. We quickly became accustomed to flying perhaps a heavy bomber, a high-performance fighter and a light trainer all in one day, sometimes a jet, sometimes a propeller aircraft.

Accommodation in the Farnborough area was almost impossible to find, so Sally and I had a caravan built to our own design and in this we made a warm and comfortable home until the course ended in December 1952.

There were 33 pilots in my year, No. 11 Course. Although the majority were from the RAF, there were six officers from the Royal Navy, two from the United States Navy, one from the United States Air Force and one from the Indian Air Force. We formed a congenial group and many lasting friendships were made. Although flying accidents were common amongst test pilots in those days, we were perhaps fortunate to suffer not more than two fatalities whilst at Farnborough. Several of our fellow students, and some of the instructing staff, were former members of Bomber Command, whose aircrew had so inspired us by their supreme courage and endurance in repeated night assaults deep into enemy airspace whilst themselves suffering fearsome losses.

Those of us who had been accustomed to flying high-performance fighter aircraft had little difficulty coping with the four-engined bombers and the airliners, but those pilots who had a heavy aircraft background found the fighters, especially those driven by a single piston engine, an unaccustomed handful to manage. The propeller driven Sea Fury, in particular, with its one powerful engine, developed very high levels of torque. Flying this proved an alarming experience for some.

On the course with me was an old friend, Flight Lieutenant R.E. (Tick) Tickner. He had been a fellow student several years before on the Flying Instructors' course at RAF Little Rissington in Gloucestershire. Like many other wartime RAF pilots whom I much admired, he was excellent and amusing company throughout our time at Farnborough and, together with our wives, we maintained a firm friendship for years afterwards. He shared my interest in fly-fishing, and in later years at the village of Wylye, where his cottage bordered the river, fresh trout was regularly on the menu.

One fine morning in May I was making a test climb to high altitude in a twin-engined Meteor jet fighter. This aircraft was not pressurised, and somewhere between 20,000 and 30,000 feet I began to feel unwell. In a very hazy and uncertain way, whilst continuing my climb, I sensed that I was not in proper control of the aircraft.

100

Then, unaccountably, I found myself at a much lower altitude than I had been previously. I felt no compulsion or even the slightest need to explain what had occurred, for I had no sense that anything was unusual. My oxygen flow instrument indicated that oxygen was flowing correctly, but again I became aware in a vague sort of way that things were not as they should be. I could not understand the strange feelings I was experiencing and I decided to visit the doctor after the flight. Not realising that I was only partly conscious, I resumed my climb and, once more reaching high altitude, I again lost consciousness. The next thing I knew was that the aircraft was rolling about its longitudinal axis in almost level flight at 12,000 feet. In my befuddled state I slowly realised that I had a serious problem and I returned at once to Farnborough and landed, soon developing a most severe headache.

When the aircraft was inspected it was found that the oxygen supply pipe had not been connected below the pilot's seat. Although oxygen was flowing, it was not passing into the tube leading to the pilot's mask. The Meteor's control surfaces had been adjusted by trimming devices to maintain a steady flight path. Climbing power was applied and one can only wonder at what extraordinary manoeuvres it must have made during my long periods of unconsciousness. If the aircraft had remained at high altitude instead of losing height I would not now be writing this account and the loss of a fighter and its pilot would have been just another unexplained disaster in the history books. How fortunate I was – but was it good luck or did a guardian angel take control and bring my aircraft down to a safe altitude and into almost level flight?

Oxygen systems were later changed from this constant flow system to one called the 'Demand System', in which oxygen flows only when the pilot breathes in, with an instrument showing when oxygen is actually entering the mask.

Although the universal Ground Controlled Approach Radar (GCA) system had not at this time been fully developed, Farnborough had set up its own unique approach aid, which it named Precision Approach Radar (PAR). It was generally very helpful but it was not without imperfections. One dark November evening with visibility down to just a few hundred yards, I was returning to base after a test flight in a large four-engined Lincoln bomber. As usual my crew consisted solely of a flight engineer. Farnborough Control was bringing me in on an instrument approach using PAR. At the end of the approach the Controller gave me the customary instruction to 'look ahead and land'. When I looked ahead there was no runway to be seen but, looking down, I saw the runway lights far below me. It was such a foul night that I was not willing to go round and try again so, cutting all engines, I brought her down like a Tiger Moth and, with screaming brakes, just avoided running off the end of the runway.

Back at the squadron office I received a summons to report to Wing Commander Flying in the control tower. His opening comment was, 'My God, Shaw, it's just as well we've got a long runway, isn't it?'

Before I could open my mouth to answer my flight engineer said, 'Why do you say that, sir? We only used one quarter of it!' Even the Wing Commander could not hold back a laugh and this ended the matter. My already high opinion of flight engineers was thus raised still further.

During my period at Farnborough a landing arrester-gear with a flexible rubber deck was set up on the airfield. It was designed as an experiment to examine the possibility of operating fighter aircraft with no landing wheels from carriers. The undercarriage and its associated hydraulic systems are heavy and require much space internally, and it was proposed that an aircraft without this encumbrance could be launched by catapult and would have a greatly superior performance. A Vampire jet, having no propeller, was chosen for the trial. Its belly was specially strengthened to allow it to make wheels-up landings on the rubber deck and the naval pilots on my course each participated in the trials. Using a novel approach technique, I made four rubber deck landings. The aircraft withstood the shocks, though it was a bone-shaking experience for the pilot as the aircraft made several leaps on the rubber before coming to a stop. One aircraft carrier was fitted with a rubber deck for experimental purposes but the project was dropped.

The test pilots' course was demanding of its students but it was not all work and no play. During the year we made three week-long visits to firms in the aircraft industry. A region of Britain was chosen where we spent time at a number of companies making airframes, engines, propellers, hydraulic machinery and other component parts. We toured the departments, met the test pilots and attended lectures by prominent members of staff. In the evenings we were treated to the most generous hospitality, memorably a cruise on the Thames followed by dinner at a fine riverside hotel on the Hawker company, a night in Blackpool on English Electric (makers of the Canberra), dinner and a variety theatre in the Midlands on Lucas, and an evening at the Festival of Britain in London to name a few. The hospitality was such that concentrating on work the following day required great dedication.

At the Hawker Aircraft company at Dunsfold the management had lined up three historic aircraft for us to fly: a Hurricane, a Hart and a Tomtit. With plenty of Hurricane hours in my 1943 log-book, I decided to select one of the earlier-type biplanes. I chose the Tomtit and, in perfect weather, enjoyed 30 minutes of flying as it was in the days between the wars.

With the year drawing to a close the pace of work rose to a peak. We sat our final examinations in December 1952 and celebrated our success with the receipt from the Commandant of the coveted certificate confirming our graduation as Experimental Test Pilots from the Empire Test Pilots' School. A last dinner signalled our departure from Farnborough to await appointments to our next jobs.


After a week or two of leave with Sally, by now in the last stages of pregnancy with our first child, I reported to the Aircraft and Armaments Experimental Establishment at Boscombe Down, where I was to spend the next two years. I joined 'C' Squadron, the Naval Test Squadron, which was exceptionally busy coping with the demands of the Fleet Air Arm for the modern aircraft and weapons required by our carriers operating in the Far East during the Korean War. We had our caravan home moved to Boscombe Down and set it up on a site specially allocated to officers where many other pilots were already established with their families.

In the Navy Test Squadron I found my old friend Peter 'Sheepy' Lamb as Senior Pilot. During the war years we had trained together, flown together in No. 4 Wing for two years and qualified together as 'batsmen' at the end of 1944. Thereafter our paths had diverged. Sheepy was a robust character, a great shipmate and a lifelong friend.

For much of my time at Boscombe Down my squadron Commanding Officer was Commander Stan Orr. He had an enviable war record and strong, sound and well-thought-out views on how the Fleet Air Arm should develop. With his amusing and delightful personality he inspired great loyalty and respect from those he led. I had known him previously as our Wing Leader in HMS *Indomitable* and, if promotion could have been determined by those who served under him, I believe he would have risen to the highest ranks in the Service.

When Sally's term was almost up she went to her parents' home at Rowledge and, on 28th January 1953, at a maternity home in Wrecclesham, our first son was born. Despite pressure of work, my CO granted me 12 hours off to visit my family and, joy of joys, to find mother and child in flourishing health and to name our son Christopher. As all parents will understand, this was a great moment of my life.

At the squadron we were working seven days a week, often for months at a time. None of our aircraft at that period was able to fly at supersonic speed. None, in fact, could get close to the speed of sound without becoming uncontrollable. Flying controls were not at that time able to cope with the shockwaves and flutter problems which developed at high speed and much of our work involved observing the behaviour of airframes and engines at mach numbers approaching one.

As well as examining the flying characteristics and performance of the aircraft as flying machines, we carried out lengthy trials of the weapon systems; studying the behaviour of the plane under all variations of bomb loads, and the operation of the cannon and machine-gun systems.

Not long after joining 'C' Squadron I was making my first flight in a prototype swept-wing fighter codenamed N7/46, designed as a successor to the Hawker Seahawk. Returning to base on completion of my task, I was unable to lower my undercarriage. The starboard wheel and the nosewheel lowered satisfactorily but the port wheel remained locked up in its housing. The non-offending wheels retracted again correctly, but after operating the system in all manner of evolutions, including inverted flight, the port wheel stubbornly refused to unlock. To operate the emergency lowering system was now the only option. This was a pneumatic system designed to blow the wheels down but, once used, the hydraulics were cut out and the undercarriage could not again be raised. With the agreement of the controller in the tower, I operated the emergency system. To my dismay this failed to budge the port leg, with the result that I was committed to a one-up, one-down landing. A bale-out was the only other possibility but this meant the loss of a prototype aircraft and was not a realistic choice.

While I circled Boscombe Down to burn off fuel, the runway was selected which gave the greatest possible cross-wind from starboard, and the fire and ambulance services positioned themselves in appropriate places.

It was in these circumstances that I made my first ever landing in this new, unproven aircraft. After touch-down I held it straight until the port wing dropped and made contact with the runway when, of course, directional control was lost. The fighter then performed a neat and tightening curve across the grass on port wing-tip and nosewheel. There was a fear that it might cartwheel if the wing dug in, but fortunately this did not occur. The emergency services had been rather too well placed, however, and vehicles began to scatter in all directions as I approached. It became clear to me that I would 'get' one of them, and it turned out to be the ambulance. It was making a rapid retreat when I struck it just behind the cab, moving the vehicle bodily sideways a considerable distance, to the alarm of the driver and medic sitting next to him. The nose of my aircraft was firmly embedded in the bodywork.

The aircraft was not seriously damaged and, in due course, it was repaired, but the ambulance was a total write-off and fit only for scrap, to the great joy of the Principal Medical Officer, a Wing Commander. He came to see me the following day with a hugely satisfied grin on his face and thanked me profusely, saying that he had been trying for years, without success, to obtain a replacement for his out-of-date vehicle. Already, he said, a brand new ambulance was on its way to Boscombe, and he would be forever grateful to the Fleet Air Arm for such a worthwhile accident.

I was taken to sick-bay for a check-up and was found unharmed and fit. The ambulance driver and his mate were, however, suffering from shock and were detained for treatment. Apart from this small matter it had been, particularly for the PMO, a most happy and rewarding occasion.

105

*   *   *

My two years at Boscombe Down involved much routine test flying and report writing but, as for any pilot, certain tasks and events stand out in my memory. Navy test pilots, unlike their counterparts in the RAF, must assess the suitability and performance of their aircraft when operating not just from airfields and landing grounds, but from carriers at sea. Thus I was involved in day and night carrier trials of several types, including the Sea Venom night fighter, and even day carrier landing trials with a Meteor twin-jet fighter which had been specially fitted with an arrester hook.

During my first year in 'C' Squadron I was largely occupied with the development of the Hawker Seahawk, a single-seat fighter. The work was always demanding and never dull, usually requiring total concentration. The test programme proceeded month after month until the spinning trials commenced. I was allotted the high-altitude trials to be made from 30,000 feet. As I contemplated the prospect I repeated to myself the old saying, 'If you can't take a joke you shouldn't have joined.' Each spin was to be held for four full turns before recovery action was taken.

Putting a high-performance aircraft deliberately into a spin and holding it there is, I believe, not something that any right-minded pilot would do for pleasure, but it was part of the test programme and I had been given the task of carrying it out. At high altitude the Seahawk, held into the spin, performed the most extraordinary antics, with the nose sometimes rearing up to near vertical and then flicking and plunging down steeply, but it always recovered when the correct action was applied. The trials required that spins be made in each direction under all sorts of different control and airframe configurations, pro and anti aileron, flaps in various settings, undercarriage up and down and combinations of all these. Thus the programme extended over several weeks and I was more than pleased when it was completed.

Many were the flights we made to the gunnery and bombing ranges in Lyme Bay, to the south of Lyme Regis, to prove the operation of the cannon, machine-gun and rocket systems of the fighter aircraft, and to test the procedures for rearming them on the ground. When an armaments programme was in full flow we made sortie after sortie out to the ranges, fired our weapons, returned for reloading, then took off to repeat the procedure again and again

106

in a series lasting all day, or maybe several days. As well as undergoing gunnery trials, the aircraft were tested in the fighter-bomber role. Bomb-release systems were tested and these trials, too, were carried out over the waters off Lyme Regis. The handling and the performance of the aircraft when carrying bombs was investigated, and this included the flying characteristics after a bomb suffered a 'hang-up' under one wing. The take-off was made with two bombs, one under each wing. Over the range one bomb was released and the handling of the aircraft was examined with this asymmetric load.

The Seahawk was a particularly attractive aircraft with very beautiful lines. I grew to love it although not every flight in it was a pleasure. One winter night it gave me probably the most hazardous and one of the most unforgettable experiences of my flying career.

A trial was ordered to examine the behaviour of the aircraft under conditions of extreme cold. The pilot was required to climb to 35,000 feet after midnight and to remain there for as long as possible with no heating, and with just enough power to maintain height. The Seahawk was not pressurised and 35,000 feet was the greatest height at which it was safe to remain whilst breathing pure oxygen. A suitable night was chosen at dead of winter and it fell to my lot to undertake the trial. Having dressed in the warmest clothing I could lay my hands on, it was only with difficulty that I managed to get inside the outer layer, my flying suit. When comfortably ensconced in the cockpit, I set off for the runway, took off, and made my climb to altitude. Once established in level flight with minimum power, I settled down to a long and tedious patrol over southern England. After half an hour or so the cockpit temperature, which I recorded every five minutes, had stabilised at minus 62°C. Despite the extra layers of clothing I was wearing, the cold soon penetrated into my very bones. The time passed agonisingly slowly and, as my body seemed gradually to freeze, I could think only of my friends – all of England, in fact – asleep in their warm beds seven miles below.

At last the long misery came to an end and I began the descent for my return to base. Then, while I was losing height, suddenly, without any warning, my windscreen shattered. Being laminated, it remained in position, but all forward vision was lost. Luckily the side panels were unaffected, so that I could see out on either beam and, by constantly banking the aircraft, I was able to find my way back to the airfield at Boscombe Down.

No sooner had I adjusted to this problem than my airspeed indicator failed. This, added to my loss of vision, confounded the problem of making a safe approach and landing. Indication of airspeed was important to the pilot, especially during the circuit when landing gear and flaps were lowered, and when the final approach was made. Fortunately I had flown the Seahawk for sufficient hours to know its handling characteristics well. With more than a little apprehension I made my circuit, using engine revolutions as a guide to the appropriate moment to lower the undercarriage and flaps. I relied on the 'feel' of the aircraft to judge its approach speed. Boscombe gave me the best available airfield lighting as I made the only possible manoeuvre under the circumstances, a steeply banked turning approach to a landing. Though dangerous, with no indication of airspeed, this method enabled me to see the runway lights through the side panel. Straightening up at the last moment I made my landing and, with faith, hope and a lot of luck, I managed to stay on the runway as the lights flashed past on either side.

Coming to a stop, I encountered a new problem: the cockpit canopy would not open – it remained firmly locked shut. With no forward vision I could not taxi back to dispersal, so I was instructed to shut the engine down and await the arrival of a recovery vehicle to tow me back to the squadron. There the ground crew were able to release my canopy and to lift me from the cockpit, my body stiff with the cold, and still shivering.

Once in the warm crew room with a steaming coffee, I slowly came back to working order, though this could certainly not be said of my aircraft. Later I was told that valuable lessons had been learnt and I was more than gratified, and relieved, when I was informed that I would not be asked to repeat that particular trial.


Eight different types of aircraft were undergoing tests during my time at Boscombe Down and I took part in trials of all of them. Amongst them were the Fairey Gannet, the Westland Wyvern, the Boulton Paul Balliol and the Short Seamew. In my second year, I became chiefly concerned with the De Havilland Sea Venom, a two-seat version of the RAF Venom single-seat fighter. It was designed to operate as a naval night fighter, to replace the piston-engined Firefly.

The Korean War was at its height and there was an urgent demand by the Navy for a more modern carrier-based night fighter. The need was so pressing that there was not time to produce a totally new purpose-built aircraft – hence the search for an existing jet fighter which could be converted to the two-seat, radar-carrying, role. The Venom was chosen, and the Sea Venom was developed to carry a pilot and an observer side by side behind a flat windscreen. Like the Venom, it had twin booms, each with a fin, supporting a single wide tailplane.

It had not been possible at that time to install ejection seats. A special design was required to enable two of them to fit into the cockpit and to add an associated mechanism for prior ejection of the canopy. The cockpit was pressurised to make high-altitude operation safe and more comfortable for the crew, especially at night.

During the months I spent on trials of the Sea Venom I developed a deep distrust of the type, and the more I and my colleagues became aware of its shortcomings, the more I felt it was unsuitable for its task. On two occasions at high altitude my aircraft suffered an explosive decompression when a cockpit quarter panel blew out. This was a somewhat alarming experience as it happened so suddenly and without any warning. My flight observer on one of these occasions was a bearded man. Before we could get down to a lower altitude and land back at base, his frozen whiskers gave him the look of an Antarctic explorer.

Lateral control at low speed was very poor and quite inadequate for the approach to a landing on board an aircraft carrier, so a special gearing system had to be devised and fitted to the aileron control to overcome this problem. The slab windscreen became obscured by rain water at low speeds and various methods of overcoming this were tried, none totally successful. With no ejection seats, the chance of a safe bale-out by the crew in emergency was slim, not least because of the wide stabiliser at the tail. It was known that, if the aircraft was landed in the sea, the booms would break off, resulting in the cockpit area plunging steeply. Here was a naval night fighter with poor control, poor visibility in rain, from which the crew could neither bale out nor ditch. This was not a combination to inspire confidence amongst squadron aircrews in the future.

Whilst I was making the night deck-landing trials it was impossible not to be conscious of these shortcomings. In reports and discussions at the Ministry our feelings about this aircraft were stressed, but political pressures took priority and the Sea Venom was brought into service – though by then ejection seats had been installed and some other improvements had been made. Nevertheless, one of my oldest and best friends was amongst those killed when operating these aircraft from carriers.

*Chapter 12*

# *To the New World (1955–7)*

One day I was informed by my CO that I had been selected to fill an exchange appointment with a fighter development squadron of the US Navy at a base in New Jersey. The experimental squadron VX–3 was working on aircraft and equipment more advanced than anything our navy had at that time. The prospect was an exciting one. Sally and two-year old Christopher would accompany me and we would live and work as members of an American squadron.

Before leaving the UK I was appointed as Officer-in-Charge Flying at the newly constructed Royal Aircraft Establishment at Bedford, where an experimental aircraft arrester gear had been installed and was ready for tests. With a team of several pilots and a wide selection of aircraft, we spent hours and hours over many weeks engaging the arrester wires over a widening range of speeds and weights. The gear proved most reliable and capable of coping with the high landing speeds and the heavy weights of the forthcoming generation of naval aircraft. It was soon to be installed as standard equipment in our carriers.

In February 1955 Sally, Christopher and I embarked in the *Queen Mary* at Southampton where, in her glistening paintwork, the great liner was berthed at Ocean Terminal. Both sets of parents came to see us off. They were able to accompany us on board, to view the public rooms, admire our cabin and join us for a meal before we sailed that evening.

The balconies of the Ocean Terminal were alive with waving arms and fluttering streamers as slowly we moved away from the dockside, the traditional farewell to the world's most famous liner. How different this was from the wartime departure for the USA I

111

had made in a drab troopship 13 years earlier when heading across a U-boat-infested Atlantic for my flying training.

With gathering speed we moved towards the Solent and, as sight of the terminal was lost, our great adventure began. And what a start it was, the luxury of the *Queen Mary*, the incomparable food, the excitement of getting away from the cold English winter, from the rationing and shortages. It was all overwhelming. A spell of severe weather caused even our great ship to slow down. This delayed our arrival in New York and we were delighted to have six days aboard instead of the usual five. Christopher was happily occupied during the days and, with baby-sitters at night, we were able to enjoy to the full the wonderful amenities on board. We lived in a dream world which we wished would go on for ever but, sadly, it had to come to an end. We docked in New York and made our way by train to Atlantic City where, at Pomona airfield, VX–3 was based.

So began an intensely interesting two-and-a-half years living and working as an American, enjoying the 'good life' quite unknown to us in the austerity of Britain at that time. After my return from the Pacific war in 1946 I had put my name down for a new car at the main Vauxhall agent in our nearby town of Andover. It was just a small family saloon but when we left for the States my name had still not reached the top of the waiting list, eight years later! After moving into a rented house on the island of Brigantine, our first priority was therefore to buy a car. This was simplicity itself and in two days we were the proud owners of a brand new gleaming Ford saloon. What a contrast from the circumstances prevailing in Britain.

Sally quickly made friends with our neighbours and with the many squadron wives who lived nearby on the island. There were numerous children amongst these families and in no time Christopher was enjoying their company and rapidly becoming a real little Yankee. The beach on the ocean side of the island was sandy and safe for swimming and was a joy for the youngsters. The friendly and welcoming families were ready with all the advice Sally needed, and soon we settled to our new life in this land of plenty.

We soon discovered that any household goods which we needed could ideally be obtained from the great American institution of Sears Roebuck. An easy journey of some 70 miles in our new car took us to a major branch of Sears in the historic city of Philadelphia.

At our first encounter with this store we were spellbound by the vast display of products for the home, the garden, the workshop and for sporting and leisure activities. After the shortages and rationing in Britain this huge shopping emporium was unlike anything we had known before, or even dreamed of. It was a dazzling experience and the things that we bought there were of high quality. Now, 45 years later, we still enjoy our household china and kitchenware from Sears Roebuck and their fine tools are in constant use in my workshop.

In Philadelphia we were introduced to a waterside restaurant, The Old Original Bookbinders. This became our favourite eating place whenever we were able to visit the great city. The finest lobster, cooked and served in unique style, was the irresistible attraction, and memories of those happy occasions still linger. I hope the Old Original still prospers.


VX–3 Squadron was commanded by a Captain US Navy and comprised 60 officers, mostly pilots, many of whom were graduates of the Navy Test Pilots' School at Patuxent River. A varied range of fighter aircraft were undergoing all sorts of experimental and development trials. We worked hard by day and night, both ashore and afloat aboard carriers. Within a week or so of joining I had made my first supersonic flight, something I had been working towards for years in Britain but had never achieved! It was ironic that the aircraft in question was powered by a British engine, the Armstrong Siddeley Sapphire. This only served to emphasise the gap in pace of advance between our two countries in the development of airframes and control systems. The large funds available to support the design and production of new aircraft and equipment was staggering to me, coming from Britain, where great constraints on expenditure prevailed.

As a general rule the week's work ended on Friday evening and 'happy hour' at the officers' club was the prelude to a weekend of serious play. The good climate, the beaches, the water sports in the sheltered bay, the barbecues, the private parties all filled our time.

During my service in VX–3 I took part in many different trials, and flew many types of advanced aircraft faster and higher (52,300 feet) than ever before. For my work on carrier operations with the angled deck and the mirror landing sight I was most gratified, and surprised, to receive a commendation from the United States Navy.

The trials of the angled deck design for landing aircraft aboard carriers, together with the day and night assessment of the mirror landing aid, were completed on board carriers within the Atlantic fleet. It was then decided to duplicate the examination of the two systems within the Pacific Fleet. The trials were to be undertaken aboard the USS *Antietam*, a large carrier which had been modified structurally to incorporate the new developments. The ship was to operate out of the great naval base at San Diego, and the aircraft and their crews from its associated Naval Air Station at North Island.

I was despatched from Squadron VX–3 to fly to California to assist in the arrangements for the trials and to brief all concerned on the workings of the two systems, and in the recommended ways of using them. This presented me with a significant opportunity to explain the advantages of these British inventions and, at the same time, to see something of the legendary state of California. Whilst ashore in San Diego I was accommodated in considerable comfort at the North Island Officers' Club, where it was customary to take a buffet lunch in the sunshine at the poolside. Mexican food was very popular, the national border being only a few miles to the south. My first genuine chilli con carne came as a severe shock and seemed to take my head off, but in days to come I grew to enjoy the fire which was ignited within me at each meal.

When the opportunity arose I took the 14-hour journey by Greyhound bus to Yosemite Valley and stayed there overnight in a log cabin. The magnificence of this natural gorge with its high mountains rising sheer from a green and wooded valley, and with its mighty waterfalls cascading thousands of feet to the river below, is one of the glories of the West. It makes a stunning impact on the visitor, who can but marvel at such grandeur.

Back at North Island I was invited by friends one Sunday to accompany them to Tijuana on the Mexican border to witness a bullfight. I approached this with some enthusiasm as I had never before seen such a spectacle, but with the first bull lying dead upon the sand of the arena, I was ready to return forthwith to California. However, being dependent upon my friends for transport, I had no option but to witness the torture and death of five more superb animals. I have to admit that the moment of entry of the fearsome and magnificently powerful bull was thrilling and electrifying, but thereafter I found the process sickening.


Whilst I served in VX–3 the USA was entering the early planning stages for the exploration of space using rockets carrying capsules manned by especially trained astronauts. All sorts of engineering problems had to be solved in the construction of spacecraft to enable them to withstand the forces and temperatures that would be encountered at launch and recovery. The capsule had to be pressurised, heated and have an appropriate atmosphere for the crew, who needed specially designed suits for survival. The capsule needed facilities to allow the crew to eat, drink, work, sleep and perform their natural functions. Such enormous problems must at times have seemed insurmountable, but scientists and engineers, with the necessary incentives and with huge government support, were determined to succeed, however unfavourable the odds might be.

In order to examine and establish the limits of G-forces which could be tolerated by the human body, the Aviation Medical Acceleration Laboratory had built the world's largest human centrifuge at the US Naval Air Development Centre at Johnsville, Pennsylvania. Naval Air squadrons, including VX–3, were asked to seek volunteers to subject themselves to a programme designed to determine the maximum level of G-force that could be withstood, and for how long it could be sustained. The pilot sat in a capsule on the end of a long arm, which was then rotated at increasing speed until a desired and steady G-force was attained. This steady force was maintained as long as the pilot remained conscious. A simple, but ingenious, method was employed to indicate unconsciousness. The pilot had a button with which he could switch off a red light situated before him in the capsule. He watched the light, and every time it came on he was required to switch it off. When he failed to do so he was deemed to be unconscious. Each volunteer made a series of runs at gradually increasing levels of G-force, and the time he was able to remain conscious at each level was recorded.

Some months later, when all the trial results had been analysed, I was informed that I held the record for the time spent at 7-G before consciousness was lost. However, about a year later Johnsville told me that my record still stood for all the aviators who had been tested, but that it had since been beaten by a United States Navy seaman rating. I wondered if, consequently, he suffered the same rear-end malady that I did, a trouble commonly known amongst aviators as 'fighter pilot's disease'. If so, that seaman may justifiably feel proud!

I regarded my United States Navy test squadron colleagues as a group of courageous individuals. They were involved in a multitude of development projects, some of which were extremely hazardous. A can-do attitude pertained throughout the squadron which, in my time, was commanded by Captain Robert Dose, a much decorated naval officer with a distinguished war record. Outwardly he came across as a man-of-iron and he was assuredly not a person that anyone would be wise to cross. However, as I came to know him well, and to admire him, I found that he had a soft, kindly and most generous heart. He and his wife, Betty, have ever since been among our greatest friends. They have stayed with us in Britain and we have several times spent happy holidays with them at their lovely home at La Jolla, near San Diego.

On one of our trips to California Bob and Betty gave us the use of their cottage at Borrego Springs, an oasis of lush green and flower-strewn beauty in the midst of the burning solitude of the Borrego Desert. Lying at the foot of a range of bare and rugged mountains, this haven of peace and sunshine is set with swimming pools, tennis courts and golf courses. Everywhere are close-mown lawns bordered by exotic and colourful shrubs and flowers. To us this was the American good life in its ultimate form. For me, however, more wonderful than all this ease and comfort was the desert surrounding the Springs. In Bob's four-wheel-drive Toyota, which he had given us to use for our holiday, we drove each day out into this golden land of sand, rugged hills and rocky outcrops. We learnt the names of the multitude of cactus and marvelled at their range of strange and subtle forms. We searched in vain for Bighorn sheep and, as we had been advised, watched out for rattlesnakes, and for flash floods in the event of a sudden storm.

The utter silence of the desert was intense. We felt we could hear it, so accustomed were we to the background noise ever-present in our modern world. Those days spent in the remoteness of the desert had a deep and moving effect upon me. I had always believed that the poet spoke the absolute truth when he wrote 'You are nearer to God in a garden than anywhere else on earth'. Now I think that the desert is, perhaps, even more deserving of those sentiments.

Apart from being answerable to the US Navy Captain for my duties as a member of an American squadron, I was answerable, as well, to the Naval Air Staff Officer in the British Services Mission in Washington. For much of my appointment with VX–3 my British boss in the capital was Commander George Baldwin, an old friend and shipmate who had been, first, a squadron commander and, later, my wing leader for two years during the war. He built up a good working relationship with the Captain and officers of VX–3, and from time to time he paid us a visit to fly some of the fighter planes we had under development. He and his wife, Hasle, invited us several times to stay with them in Washington, so giving us the opportunity to explore the city and admire its magnificent buildings and museums, and to see something of the local countryside. In the summer months, when the intense heat and humidity of Washington became insufferable, they took opportunities to come across to the New Jersey shore and stay with us on our island of Brigantine. There they could enjoy sea breezes and swimming in the ocean from our sandy beaches. Another Fleet Air Arm colleague, Murray Hayes, was on exchange in the USA at the same time as me. He was working on the development of helicopters with another United States Navy experimental squadron, at Key West on the southern tip of Florida. To pay each other a visit with our families was a convenient excuse to see a bit more of our host country.

Sally loved the life and Christopher grew up strong and healthy. Our second child was on the way before we completed our tour, but his birth was not to be early enough for him to be born an American citizen. We had made many lasting friendships, and survived the month-long series of leaving parties. Then it was with sadness that we departed in the summer of 1957 to return home.

We joined the *Queen Elizabeth* at Halifax, Nova Scotia, to enjoy once again the matchless comfort and pleasure of a transatlantic voyage in one of the world's greatest ocean liners. As we sailed away I reflected upon the good fortune I had encountered in my various associations with the generous people of the United States.

117

In 1942 they had given me my flying training and had presented me with US Navy wings. Two years later fighting soldiers of the US Army had, at loss to themselves, given me back my freedom when they liberated the French town of Grignan, where I was hiding from the Germans. Now, for more than two years, I and my family had delighted in the life we led in their vast and magnificent country, in the demanding work of Squadron VX–3 and, above all, in the many friends we had made. I had good cause to feel much gratitude to that great nation.

## Chapter 13

# Another Side of the Navy (1957–8)

Soon after our return to the United Kingdom Sally entered the Royal Military Hospital Aldershot for the birth of our second son, George. I was serving in the cruiser *Gambia* based at Rosyth in Fife. My Captain, 'Dusty' Dunsterville, gave me a couple of days' leave to travel south to make the acquaintance of the new addition to our family. I had the joy of finding both mother and son doing well and I held the warm, pink baby in my arms for a wonderful but brief period before I had to return by train to Scotland.

*Gambia* was working up in Scottish waters before sailing for the Far East, where she was to fly the flag of the C-in-C East Indies Station. For me it was to be my first non-flying appointment since I joined the Navy 16 years earlier. Apart from watchkeeping on a regular basis I was to do spells of duty in the main seaman departments of the ship. *Gambia* was an 8,000-ton cruiser of the Colony class with a main armament of 12 six-inch guns in four triple turrets. Her complement of about 50 officers and over 600 men made for a sizeable community. She carried a secondary armament of 26 anti-aircraft guns.

Sally drove to Scotland with Christopher and young George to stay at a guesthouse in North Queensferry for a few weeks before we left Rosyth at the end of our work-up. On a fine Sunday morning in *Gambia*'s lovely chapel, George was baptised by our chaplain, the Rev. Kenneth Evans. We sailed for the Far East in October 1957 after giving families a day at sea. Sally came aboard with the two boys. Christopher had the run of the ship with several other youngsters of similar age whilst George, the youngest member present, passed the day in his carrycot on the bunk in my cabin. Sally and I were guests at the Captain's luncheon party. During

119

our two-and-a-half years on exchange appointment in the United States I had picked up quite a number of Americanisms and a bit of an accent. After lunch the Captain remarked to me, 'I have to say, Tony, your wife has it worse than you!'

During the following 16 months I was to be Forecastle and Cable Officer, Communications Officer, Navigating Officer, Entertainments Officer and responsible for a division of sailors. For the period of the work-up I was given the job of Forecastle Officer. With no previous experience of this work, I had to learn quickly the procedures for dropping anchor, weighing anchor, mooring ship and all the customary processes involved in leaving and entering harbour. The ratings of the 'Cable Party' were under the management of a very experienced seaman petty officer. I relied upon him entirely and he was only too pleased to put me right in all the secrets of the trade. Over a period of a few weeks I became expert at controlling the great anchor cables, and doing so without losing fingers, feet, legs or life itself. Such massive ironmongery rushing at breakneck speed across the deck when dropping anchor was a frightening sight, and made an awe-inspiring noise. I felt that handling all this heavy metal was one of the most satisfying things I had ever done.

The work-up programme required us to make many early morning starts from Rosyth dockyard. Once the ship was under way the Forecastle Officer's post was right up at the very forward tip of the bows – in 'the eyes of the ship'. Standing up there on a winter's morning, passing under the Forth Bridge and past the flag saluting station in an icy blast of wind was a freezing, eye-watering experience and, when I had done it for the first time, I realised why I, as a green new boy, had been given the job of Forecastle Officer for the initial period of our commission in North Sea waters. That's the funny side of life, and I enjoyed every minute of it!

Our passage to the Persian Gulf was made through the Mediterranean and the Suez Canal. Life on board was full of interest for me, and much in contrast to my experience in aircraft carriers. Totally absent was the atmosphere of stress and noise which prevailed in carriers, where the hazards and dangers of operations by day and night were ever-present.

In general, work proceeded at a gentle and steady pace and I found myself relaxing and enjoying this unaccustomed way of life. I rapidly settled into the various and absorbing roles I was given in the business of running the ship. As a pilot accustomed to being alone in the air and making decisions without help, it was a revelation to find that when problems arose there were always experts readily to hand from whom to seek advice.

As the flagship, we made official visits to numerous places within the East Indies Station: Aden, the Gulf, the Horn of Africa, India, Pakistan, Ceylon (now Sri Lanka) and, most entrancing of all, the Maldive Islands. Visits lasted five or seven days and the periods at sea which followed were necessary to allow us to recover from the many parties given and received, and all the ceremonial functions involved in such visits by the Commander-in-Chief.

The C-in-C's official residence in Ceylon had recently been closed down and a special dispensation was granted allowing Mrs Biggs, the C-in-C's wife, to take up permanent residence on board. From time to time a couple of officers were invited to dine with the Admiral and his wife. These occasions were always enjoyed, for the Admiral was a renowned raconteur with a fund of stories. After the meal, when the Admiral retired to his study, the guests were required to play scrabble with Mrs Biggs, who was herself an expert at the game. Needless to say she usually won.

X-Gun turret had been removed and the circular deck on which it had been situated was given over to Mrs Biggs as her private outdoor 'garden'. One day during a major SEATO maritime exercise, comprising warships from the USA, India, Pakistan, Ceylon and Britain, the Admiral called a United States Navy destroyer to come alongside and transfer a hand message. With anti-submarine exercises going on, attacking aircraft roaring overhead and the ship at action stations, the American ship eased up alongside. As she did so her captain looked down from his bridge to see Mrs Biggs in a deck chair on X-Gun deck busily dressmaking and turning her hand-driven sewing machine. The captain was reported to have commented, 'These goddam Limeys – not only liquor, but women on board!'

In the beautiful island of Ceylon we were given relief from the insufferable heat of Colombo by a period of leave up-country. A shipmate and I were fortunate indeed to be invited to stay for some days on a tea plantation, owned by Charles Edwards. At around 5,000 feet up in the hills the climate was as perfect as could be imagined. His home was a picture of comfort and beauty set in gardens of luxuriant colour. Each morning, after a cup of the finest tea was brought to us by one of many servants, we fell straight into the cool water of the pool whilst the sun climbed over the hills. As we dried ourselves in the warming sunshine we looked down over the jungle-covered coastal plain to the ocean some 50 miles away.

At every port of call during our commission we put on a show by our concert party. Devised and produced by Tom Orr, the Electrical Department Commander, it was always well received and was a joy to participate in. Tom was a much experienced thespian who produced a show of near professional standard. Nothing 'blue' was permitted. Being the flagship, we enjoyed the services of a Royal Marine band. They made a huge contribution to the success of the enterprise.

After 16 months in *Gambia* this pleasurable interlude in my career came to an end. I bade a sad farewell to my Captain and shipmates and flew home to be reunited with my family and to resume my duties in the demanding world of aviation

## Chapter 14

# *Flying Again (1958–60)*

The following two years, 1958–60, were spent in Scotland. I was appointed Lieutenant Commander (Air) at the RN Air Station Abbotsinch, now Glasgow Airport. My job was head of the Air Department. A subsidiary job was CO of the RN Maintenance Test Pilots' School. Here we gave a course to pilots, often engineers, to qualify them for the testing of production aircraft prior to their despatch to user squadrons.

We worked on a range of aircraft, especially on the newly introduced twin-engined all-weather fighter, the De Havilland Sea Vixen. This well designed aircraft had most excellent systems of operation and control. It promised much potential for future development. We processed most of the factory production aircraft and despatched them to the newly forming squadrons.

Sally and I lived in a married quarter with the boys at Potter Hill, Paisley, where Christopher attended primary school and George grew up with many young friends from our neighbouring families.

Being on the outskirts of Glasgow, we were well placed to enjoy easy access to the mountains, lochs and rivers of Scotland. When weekend leave allowed we made the most of our opportunities to explore the great expanses of this magnificent country. This was always our greatest joy and, on completion of our two-year tour, we felt we had missed few chances to indulge our appetite for the most glorious scenery in all its wide variety.

At this time the Royal Navy was still deployed widely, with sizeable fleets in the Atlantic, the Mediterranean and the Far East. Since 1945 the Fleet Air Arm had established itself as the foremost instrument available to maintain the peace in distant parts of the world, or to restore it when conflicts arose. Whenever Britain felt her interests overseas to be threatened, or whenever our friends abroad sought armed help from us, it was to their naval aviators that our governments turned.

In 1960 the Royal Navy had a significant number of aircraft carriers. Their squadrons provided the main offensive power of our fleets, the early warning of an approaching enemy and the fighter protection needed. To service the initial needs of these carriers No. 700 Squadron had existed for many years and it was to command this squadron that I was next appointed.

No. 700 Squadron was based at the Royal Naval Air Station Yeovilton and, since it undertook trials of both fixed-wing and rotary-winged aircraft, it comprised experienced aircrew for each category. It was deemed desirable that the squadron commander should be at least competent on both types, to enable him to understand the problems encountered by all his pilots and to make reasoned comments upon their recommendations.

Thus it was that I headed for the Royal Naval Air Station Culdrose to undertake a helicopter pilot's course. It lasted several months and, in my case, ran through the height of the summer. Sally and the boys travelled south and set up home in a rented cottage by the sea at Praa Sands. There we enjoyed the good life afforded by the incomparable county of Cornwall – its beaches, coves and mighty flower-strewn cliffs. Whilst there we finalised plans for the purchase of our first house. We had spotted a small development of eight new homes on the outskirts of the little town of Somerton, about five miles from Yeovilton. The houses were only at the foundation stage and, by arrangement with the builder, we were able to adapt the interior to our own design.

On completion of the helicopter course we moved into our new home and, in keeping with its shape, named it Foursquare.

I assumed command of No. 700 Squadron, and during an intensively busy period we completed the deck trials of most of our aircraft carriers. As well as our British carriers we spent longish periods with the newly commissioned Brazilian Navy carrier, formerly HMS *Vengeance*, renamed the *Minas Gerais*, and with the Indian Navy's first aircraft carrier, another former British Light Fleet carrier, renamed the *Vikrant*.

Known as the Service Trials Unit, No. 700 Squadron's first role was to undertake tactical and functional trials of aircraft and equipment newly accepted for service use and to establish the best ways in which they should be operated. Secondly, it was to provide pilots and aircraft of a variety of operational types to embark for a week or ten days in carriers as they emerged from refit, or in brand new ships which had been commissioned for the first time. Whilst aboard for these trials periods, the squadron flew all manner of sorties to prove the satisfactory operation of the multitude of equipments used in launching aircraft, landing them back on, and handling them on the flight deck and in the hangars. For new ships' companies this was their first opportunity to work as a team in the operation of aircraft on and off the flight deck, a hazardous place at the best of times with a fully worked-up company, but doubly so in the early stages of a new commission.

In the case of the foreign carriers, we remained on board after the initial equipment-proving period to demonstrate the workings of a flying programme and to exercise the ship's direction systems. In the Brazilian ship very strong coffee was constantly available in every compartment, and the food in the wardroom was remarkably good. Our aircrew were divided between those who, from overeating, could not keep awake and those who, from drinking too much coffee, could not sleep. In the Indian ship curry was the order of the day, even for breakfast. Most of us were able to enjoy the strong exotic flavours but poor 'Bunny' Warren, one of our pilots, could not take it and, at every meal, a boiled egg was set before him.

The carrier trials periods were always a popular and welcome break from our shore-based work at Yeovilton. From the ships we undertook a busy and sometimes exciting programme and, although we were flying four or five different types of aircraft, we felt again like a first-line squadron, working closely together. When ashore we tended to be a looser group of individuals, each concentrating on his own particular project of the moment.

When doing carrier trials I always flew the fixed wing aircraft but, as time went on, I became more and more involved with helicopters, particularly the development of the prototype Westland P 531, especially designed for operations aboard smaller warships, primarily frigates. HMS *Undaunted* had a small flight deck constructed at the after end of the upper deck. She was based in Northern Ireland and we flew up to her on numerous occasions to operate from her in a range of weather conditions, with varying degrees of pitch and roll, and to test a number of different methods of securing the helicopter to the deck after landing. Obviously it was essential that the helicopter be prevented from sliding or toppling in severe winds and at adverse angles of roll. All sorts of ingenious systems were devised and tested before the best solution emerged. This development work I found intensely interesting and I became more and more absorbed in the problems of operating helicopters from small ships.

Whenever pressure of work allowed I was eager to get to my enthralling interests in woodwork, gardening and painting, all of which I inherited from my father, whose works are now treasured by his grandchildren.

The three gardens which I have developed from scratch have given me endless diversion from everyday concerns. The slow, but gradual, progress of cuttings as they matured into flourishing plants over a decade or more fascinated me. An instant garden, custom-built by a professional landscaper, would never have given me satisfaction.

Although my gardens may or may not outlive me, it is my hope that the pieces of furniture which I have made for family and friends will do so. To leave behind something sturdy, well-constructed and of good design which will give usefulness and pleasure for many years to come is my earnest hope.

Of my paintings, they have given me the joy of endless hours of effort – often frustrating, usually disappointing – but the knowledge of how difficult it is to produce a certain effect has enabled me to view great pictures with a new eye, with wonder and admiration. Everyone should have a go even if, like me, success eludes them.

## Chapter 15

# Helicopters (1960–2)

In 1961 it was decided to remove the helicopter trials from 700 Squadron at Yeovilton and to commission a new squadron, No. 771, at RNAS Portland, to concentrate exclusively on the development and tactical use of helicopters. I was appointed as commanding officer of this new squadron. We were equipped with several different types of aircraft, including the P531. I thus continued my already long involvement with trials of this helicopter/small ship association. We operated in all sorts of weather, often severe, by day and by night and gradually we developed the operational methods and tactics which were, in due course, to become standard when the P531 prototype was succeeded by the Westland Wasp, and when all small ships would be constructed to carry a helicopter as part of their main armament.

The development of the P531 was marred in July, soon after the formation of our new squadron, when one of our three prototypes, No. 333, was lost over the Channel. In normal flight, its tail rotor broke free from the boom and, without its stabilising effect, the fuselage proceeded to spin uncontrollably around the main rotor. In this manner the aircraft plunged into the sea. The pilot, Lieutenant Allen, survived but with a broken back. The observer, Lieutenant Colin McClure, was killed. The loss of these two good and experienced officers cast a shadow over our newly established squadron and was a source of much sadness amongst their many friends. As always, however, our busy programme continued throughout the summer into the following year, 1962.

In early 1962 the final small ship trials were carried out in a new frigate, HMS *Ashanti*. After a three-week period of operating by day and by night my observer, Nigel Fraser, and I manned our aircraft on the morning of 4th March to carry out the final test flight of the series. We were launched from the flight deck but almost immediately the aircraft went out of control, turned upside down and plunged into the sea. Neither of us has any clear idea as to how we escaped from the rapidly sinking craft but we both emerged and reached the surface, inflated our Mae Wests and waited for rescue by *Ashanti*'s lifeboat's crew. They very soon arrived on the scene and hauled us aboard. Although the sea in Lyme Bay at that time of year was cold our immersion suits kept us dry and warm. I felt no pain whatever at the time of impact and during the process of extricating myself from the wreckage, but I was astonished, later, to see what severe damage my 'bone dome' helmet had suffered. It was badly fractured. It was only some time later that I discovered massive bruising all over my body.

It was sad and ironic for me that, after two years of playing a leading part in this demanding project, it should have ended in this way, and on the very last of our programmed sorties. Nevertheless, neither Nigel nor I was seriously hurt and the systems for operating helicopters from small ships had been established and became universal in the Royal Navy.

When we left Scotland I wrote to the headmaster of my old school, Christ's Hospital, to ask him to recommend a preparatory school for Christopher. As a result he obtained a place at Sutton Place school in Seaford, Sussex. This was a long drive from Somerset when we visited him. We would stay overnight locally, and when we took him out for the day his invariable request was to visit Brighton pier, where he had to try out every one of the multitude of machines. I do not know how many hours we spent on that stilted 'pleasureland' but I have been left with an abiding aversion to such structures wherever I have come across them.

Later Christopher attended Wellington School and George, in due course, attended Dauntseys after several years at the excellent prep school Dumptons in Dorset.

# Chapter 16

# Troublous Times (1962–3)

HMS *Hermes*, one of our modern fleet carriers, was about to start a new commission and as my next job I was appointed Lieutenant Commander (Flying). As second in command of the Air Department I was responsible for the running of the flying programme and for the safety and efficiency of all aircraft operations on the flight deck, in the circuit and close vicinity of the ship. We carried a squadron of Scimitar day-fighter bombers, a squadron of Sea Vixen all-weather fighters, a squadron of anti-submarine Wessex helicopters and a flight of five Gannets for early warning.

Our intense flying programme made for long hours in the Flying Control bridge (Flyco) but it was rewarding and satisfying when, after working perhaps 18 or 20 hours a day, we had achieved our objectives in all respects. This was a vital and responsible job and I was determined to make a success of it. Our results certainly justified my optimism but, from the start of the commission, I was at loggerheads with my immediate boss, Commander (Air). In almost every respect I disagreed with him, and he with me, and I often felt near despair with frustration. This was a dangerous relationship in the critical field of flying operations in a big carrier. Nevertheless, we fulfilled our tasks over many months and our good safety and efficiency record alleviated the unhappy relations between him and me. We worked in the Atlantic and the Mediterranean throughout 1962 and then sailed for the Far East.

It was whilst in the Red Sea, early one fateful morning, that things came to head between me and my boss. We were about to enter a new zone of command and a Gannet was to be launched to fly to Aden to collect the Air Officer Commander-in-Chief and to fly him back to *Hermes*. He was to meet our Admiral, the Flag

129

Captain and their staffs, and inspect the ship. The pilot, who had only recently joined *Hermes*, was scheduled to make four practice deck landings before proceeding to Aden. When the aircraft was ranged ready for take-off I hesitated to launch it because, according to my calculations, it was overweight for an immediate landing. Commander (Air) became restless and ordered me to launch it. I continued to check my calculations, explaining repeatedly that the aircraft was overweight for landing.

Four times Commander (Air) gave me a direct order to launch, but I persevered in my refusal to clear the Gannet for take-off since to do so was, in my opinion, to endanger an aircraft, its crew and the men on deck. It was my job to ensure that all aircraft movements were properly and safely controlled, and the more my boss refused to take my objections into account, the more my feelings of frustration grew. Suddenly, after giving me the final peremptory order to launch, my simmering exasperation reached boiling point and my patience broke. In seething anger I stood up, threw down my headset, said to Commander (Air), 'Do it yourself!' and walked off.

Taken before the ship's Commanding Officer, Captain William O'Brien, I explained briefly why I had deliberately refused a direct order. I was put under open arrest and sent to my cabin. Later I was informed that I was to face trial by court martial for this offence, and that this would be held in Singapore when the ship reached there. I was to be flown from Aden in advance.

In Singapore I met John Le Blanc Smith, an old shipmate with whom I had served in HMS *Attacker* during the war and later, in peacetime, in HMS *Gambia* when he had been Operations Officer on the C-in-C's staff. Now a Captain, he offered to defend me on the three charges levelled against me: 'Wilful Disobedience', 'Behaving With Contempt' and 'Abandoning Post'. I told him that I wished to plead guilty to 'Behaving With Contempt' because that was exactly how I felt about my former boss, but he insisted that I plead 'Not Guilty' to all charges. I was grateful for his support.

While I awaited my trial I was fortunate to enjoy the company of Commander Harold Dean. He had been a fellow pupil with me in Peele 'A' House at Christ's Hospital. He had joined the Royal Navy direct from school as a 'Special Entry' cadet, a very competitive method of entering the service, requiring high academic qualities and leadership potential. He was serving on the staff in Singapore and, while I was there, he showed me round the island, stopping

130

for drinks at his favourite haunts. In his friendly and amusing company, and with his great support, I was helped through a difficult period in my naval career. He was a true friend and I was, and still am, more than grateful to him for giving so much of his time to sustaining my morale. It gave me great pleasure a few months later to read of his promotion to Captain.

I renewed acquaintance with another former shipmate, Dick Tibbatts who, when I served in *Gambia* had, as a Commander, been the ship's Executive Officer. At Singapore, in the rank of Captain, he was holding a naval appointment with the Malayan government. On Christmas Day he and his wife kindly invited me to join them for a celebratory dinner aboard his splendid launch in the open waters of Singapore harbour. It was an excellent meal in their warmhearted company, and in the afternoon we set off across the causeway to the stables of the Sultan of Johore. There I was put aboard one of his racehorses for a ride through the rubber plantations. Although I had been keen on riding in years past, I had always done so on a farm hack and never on a horse from a racing stable. The experience was electrifying. Sitting on the animal, I could feel the pent-up energy under me, like a coiled spring craving for release. Dick Tibbatts had always been a great and very enthusiastic horseman and I am indebted to him for this remarkable ride and, too, for the friendly support that he and his wife gave me at a time when I needed it most.

When *Hermes* arrived in Singapore I learnt from my friends on board that, after I had been put under arrest, Commander (Air) had himself launched the Gannet, which then made four deck landings. On completion it took off to commence its flight to Aden but the pilot was unable to retract the undercarriage. He therefore had to land on again and the sortie was cancelled. When the aircraft was examined it was found that the undercarriage was bent. When I learnt this I felt that all my troubles were over, and that my actions had been vindicated. I approached my court martial with considerable optimism.

When the crucial day arrived things did not turn out in my favour, however, as the court obviously felt that, whatever the provocation, there were better ways of refusing an order than by losing one's temper and acting as I did, especially as it was in front of all the staff in Flyco, both officers and ratings. I was found guilty on all three charges and sentenced to be severely reprimanded.

131

Even though I explained that one of my foremost responsibilities had been the safety of flying operations, I think the court was indifferent to the fact that, had I launched the Gannet, I would have committed a court martial offence by knowingly endangering an aircraft and its crew. I would then have been appearing before them, but on a different charge!

From Singapore I was flown home, with my hopes for promotion dashed, and feeling that my long career in the Royal Navy had come to ruin. I regretted this episode in my life especially for the disappointment and distress it had caused my family. At the same time, within myself, I felt that I had not done badly in maintaining a cool demeanour with my boss for so many difficult months before that fateful day when I lost restraint and something snapped inside me. Despite the unwelcome verdict of the court I was more than grateful for the support and encouragement which I had received from the Commanding Officers of the three main squadrons on board, and from a number of their senior pilots.

At Yeovilton I was given command of Heron Flight. Feeling very much under a cloud, I was buoyed by an amazing amount of moral support from old friends and even from many others whom I had not known before. We operated with a mixed fleet of aircraft, including a helicopter, and I was kept pleasantly busy with a multitude of tasks.

It was several months later that, one day when I was airborne, I received a radio message to return to base immediately and to report to the Captain. The Commanding Officer of RNAS Yeovilton at the time was Captain Rodney Carver. I respected him greatly, and had always found him an exceptionally kindly man with a fatherly manner. Nevertheless, a summons such as I had just received – to return at once whilst airborne in the midst of a task – was unusual to say the least and, as I flew back to Yeovilton, I could only speculate on what new trouble I was in.

Entering the Captain's office in some trepidation, I was instantly put at my ease. He handed me a letter which he had just received from the Ministry of Defence. It recorded the details of my court martial, listed the charges, the findings and the sentence, then went on to say that it had been Their Lordships' pleasure to quash the findings on all three charges. The Captain expressed his delight and told me to go and get a bottle of champagne and take the day off! I obeyed his order forthwith.

The possibility of such an outcome had never occurred to me, so this news came as an astonishing and wonderful surprise.

Whilst the children progressed at their boarding schools we enjoyed our home at Somerton, especially during the holidays when the boys joined us. In the summer of 1963, we bought a large frame tent, assembled a full set of camping gear and loaded it in, and on, our blue Mini and set off for the South of France. At Montélimar we stayed a few days with Madeleine, my wartime helper, revelling in her superb cooking and refreshing my memories by visiting the hill town of Grignan, where I had been in hiding during those exciting days in 1944. I was so happy to find that the town was little changed. The steep, narrow, winding streets and the stone buildings overhanging them had the same air of antiquity and the same warm and dusty smell that I had known some 20 years before. The barber's shop in which I had sat in the midst of a throng of German soldiers was still in business, though it was working at a leisurely pace more fitting for the delightfully quiet and sleepy town lying peacefully in the sunshine of southern France.

We proceeded to the coast, where at Cavalaire we set up our tent at a campsite close to the beach and the clean warm sea. The boys managed a handshake with General Charles de Gaulle when he made a visit to the area for the August anniversary of the amphibious invasion of the South of France. Refreshed after our days of sun, sea and the delights of Provence, we drove our Mini the length of France, and so home to Somerton and a return to work at Yeovilton.

When a great friend from the USA paid a visit to England we decided to give her as good a lunch as we could afford. She had been kindness itself to us when we lived in New Jersey whilst I was serving in the fighter development squadron, and we wished to show our appreciation by taking her to a top restaurant in London. Accordingly we booked a table at Simpson's in the Strand. Although this was going to cost what, for us, was a great deal of money, we felt that a meal there would show our pleasure at seeing her again.

Whilst we were enjoying pre-lunch drinks in the anteroom she rose to take a snapshot of Sally and me. The flash from her camera attracted the notice of the staff, one of whom came over to explain that Simpson's did not permit photography on the premises. Politely he asked her to desist. Our friend resumed her seat but made clear her feeling that this was a quite unreasonable intrusion upon her personal liberty, something which would not occur in her homeland. After a few minutes' reflection she stood up again and took another photograph. The reaction of the staff was immediate and, without further ado, we were escorted from the premises. Saddened by this, but at the same time feeling a great deal richer than I had expected to be, we proceeded to a nearby snack bar for coffee and a sandwich. To be thrown out of a rowdy public bar might be regarded as a humiliation and an experience best forgotten, but to be thrown out of Simpsons is a memory which secretly I treasure.

## Chapter 17

# *How Could They? (1966)*

During the later part of my time at Yeovilton the government under Harold Wilson called for a 'great national debate' on the way ahead for Britain's defence. The Fleet Air Arm, with its aircraft carriers, became a focus in Whitehall discussions but it seemed to me that, as a matter of concern to the public, it never even approached a national debate. This was hardly surprising as the carriers operated largely outside the realms of public awareness and, in its 'silent service' tradition, the Royal Navy did little to publicise their achievements. It became clear that Denis Healey, the Minister involved, was moving rapidly towards the abolition of the carriers and the Fleet Air Arm's high-performance aircraft. That such a radical move could even be contemplated was astonishing to all of us who had been accustomed to the call to arms whenever Britain's interests abroad were threatened. I wrote an article entitled 'Out of Sight – Out of Mind' (see Appendix A) in an endeavour to show how reckless and irresponsible such a policy would be to the safety and standing of our nation. I hoped to get the article published but, as a serving officer, I found this to be impossible.

By 1978 our carriers had been phased out and our capability to operate a balanced fleet was lost. The devastating effect this has had on Britain's ability to project power and influence overseas in the years since has illustrated the folly of the decision taken in the mid-1960s. The alarm and disbelief felt at that time by the Fleet Air Arm has been vindicated. Only in 1998 did the Ministry of Defence under a new Labour government announce its intention again to build large aircraft carriers able to operate an integrated force of modern aircraft. Work on this seems now to be progressing. Looking back at the Falklands War, one can only speculate as to how many lives might not have been lost and how many ships might not now be on the bottom of the south Atlantic if we had possessed carriers operating specialist airborne early warning aircraft. Despite the superb courage and skill of the FAA pilots, who overcame the enemy in such fearsome conditions, must we not feel shame that the Navy was driven to serve our country with such inadequate support. I have not noticed any sense of regret from those responsible.

As I made my last flights in helicopters I looked back on eight years' interesting and challenging work on these versatile aircraft. My work had never been specifically in the rescue field but I had, of course, done much training on rescue procedures and was fully qualified to put them into practice. However, the opportunity to make a real life-saving mission never came my way but I dreamed, as I suppose all helicopter pilots do, of putting an end to my financial worries by winching Aristotle Onassis up from his sinking yacht. We can all dream!

*Chapter 18*

# To Africa (1968–72)

West Africa beckoned next when, in 1968, I received an appointment as Defence Adviser to the British High Commissioner in Sierra Leone. At that time the Suez Canal was closed following the 1967 Arab–Israeli conflict. All Royal Navy ships moving to and from the Indian Ocean, the Persian Gulf, the Far East and the Beira patrols off East Africa were routed round the Cape of Good Hope and Freetown, with its magnificent harbour, had regained its former importance as a vital replenishment stop for ships making these extended voyages. In the Second World War the great harbour of Freetown was of huge importance to the allied navies as a convoy collection point and as a base for maritime patrols by ships and aircraft against German and other enemy submarines. The Royal Navy preserved its fuel storage depot and its associated oiling jetty in the peace that followed, and water and fresh provisions were available, whilst mail and stores flown out from the UK were held to await the ships' arrival. During my period as Resident Naval Officer almost 200 of our ships spent time in Freetown and my Chief Petty Officer and I were kept more than busy coping with all their requirements.

Our arrival in Freetown marked my first visit to Sierra Leone, but for Sally it was her second. In 1942 as a young schoolgirl she had been put ashore there from HMS *Corinthian* after being rescued from a lifeboat in mid-Atlantic. Together with her mother and her elder sister, Elizabeth, she was returning to Britain from the Middle East, where her father, a Royal Navy Captain, had held an advisory staff appointment with the Egyptian government. They had lived in Cairo for some years but, with Field Marshal Rommel's Afrika Korps only a few miles from Alexandria and threatening a full

137

invasion of Egypt, it was thought best to evacuate British service wives and children and give them passage home to the United Kingdom.

From Cairo they had travelled safely to Cape Town where, after a short stay, they were transshipped to the 20,000 ton Canadian Pacific liner *Duchess of Atholl*. Built in 1928 on the Clyde by the William Beardmore Company of Glasgow, she sailed the Liverpool–Montreal passenger route until the end of 1939, when she was requisitioned by the Admiralty for war service.

For almost three years, without any serious mishap, she plied the Atlantic and Indian Ocean, carrying many thousands of men and women from all three services. Her last voyage began on 3rd October 1942 at Cape Town with 830 passengers and crew aboard, including 58 women and 34 children. Among this number were 11-year-old Sally, her sister and her mother.

All was well until the early morning hours of 10th October when, in mid-Atlantic and 200 miles from Ascension Island, the ship was struck amidships on the port side by a torpedo from a German submarine, the U-178. The explosion destroyed the main engine room, killing all the staff on duty there. With a complete loss of power, and with the interior of the ship in total darkness, the vessel was brought to a stop, becoming a sitting target. In good order the passengers, all in their nightwear, were assembled at their lifeboat stations and, when a second torpedo exploded, again on the port side, the order was given to get all the women and children into the boats and lowered into the water. This had only just been done when a third torpedo struck the starboard side and the great ship began to settle. The Captain then gave the order to abandon ship and the remaining passengers and crew got away. Although four boats had been destroyed by the explosions, the remainder were adequate for the task of accommodating all hands.

The boats were kept together while all aboard gazed in horror at their dying ship as she rolled completely on to her port side and began gently to settle by the stern. In stunned silence the survivors watched as, slowly, their warm and comfortable home, with all their possessions, slipped for ever beneath the waves.

In a short time, the submarine surfaced and manoeuvred into the cluster of boats, demanding information from the survivors. Next, satisfied with the work she had done, the U-boat, like the *Duchess of Atholl*, slid quietly into the depths, leaving her victims to their fate on an empty and lonely ocean.

Before the sinking the Radio Officer had been able to transmit a distress call but, because his receiver set had been wrecked in the explosions, he could not know whether or not his message had been received by a shore station or by another ship. The boats kept together all that day and all the following night until, on 11th October, after many hours of agonising uncertainty, a Liberator maritime reconnaissance aircraft from Ascension Island flew over them. It turned and circled them, indicating that they were recognised. Later a vessel was sighted and, joy of joy, it turned and headed in their direction. The ship, HMS *Corinthian*, an armed merchant cruiser stopped to take all the survivors aboard. The injured were treated and, as would be expected, everyone received the most warm-hearted care and hospitality in *Corinthian* whilst they made their three-day voyage to a safe haven. Their wonder, relief and gratitude at such a remarkable rescue from fearful danger was unbounded.

The survivors were landed in Freetown where, after a spell of rest, they embarked in the Union Castle liner *Caernarvon Castle* and sailed without incident to the Clyde.

The distress message sent by the Radio Officer, correctly giving the ship's position, had been received by the signal station on Ascension Island and, except for those killed by the torpedo explosions, all on board were brought safely to harbour. Captain H.A. Moore of the *Duchess of Atholl* was decorated for the superb way he had managed the crisis on board following the explosions and for his exemplary control of the survivors in their boats until the moment of rescue.

Freetown was established in the late 18th century as a sanctuary for freed slaves. Groups of philanthropists founded the settlement on the coast of Sierra Leone by private purchase of lands from local paramount chiefs. The population grew steadily as more and more freed slaves were brought in from America, the West Indies and Britain. In the early 19th century Britain established civil control and, at the end of the century the country was formally declared a British colony.

With one of the world's largest deep-water harbours, positioned

139

conveniently between northern Europe and the Cape of Good Hope at the southern tip of Africa, Freetown grew in importance as a naval base, and when large mineral deposits were discovered inland, the population increased steadily to embrace merchants and businessmen from many nations. Citizens of European countries and the Lebanon predominated but those of the Indian sub-continent settled in significant numbers. Big deposits of iron ore, bauxite (for aluminium), rutile (for titanium) and, above all, diamonds were discovered in the hinterland and exploited throughout the 20th century.

Within Sierra Leone the chief indigenous tribes are the Mendes and the Temnes. Tribal influences are powerful, and with the addition of the freed slaves, Creoles and all the other nationalities who have made their permanent homes in the country there has been the potential for serious trouble. Ever since the discovery of valuable gemstones, the illegal digging of diamonds, and the ease with which they can be smuggled across the national borders of this small country, has been the source of unsettling and often violent dispute.

In 1961 Sierra Leone was granted full independence within the British Commonwealth and, for a few years, an elected government presided over a mostly peaceful country. Soon, however, the lure of easy riches proved too strong for honest governance, and corruption at all levels became deep-seated and widespread. Illegal mining and the smuggling of diamonds supplying a constant worldwide demand made it all too easy for huge personal fortunes to be amassed, the money being invested abroad in private accounts. Whilst persons of influence became extremely rich, the ordinary citizens of the country remained in extreme poverty.

The temptation to remove from power those who had made their fortunes proved irresistible, and a series of governments, sometimes military, sometimes civil, took over following revolutions by force of arms. Accusations of corruption were made to justify these coups but, once established, the fresh regimes found the same opportunities for profiteering.

Freetown is blessed with extensive sandy beaches washed by the warm waters of the southern Atlantic. A range of mountains extends for 30 miles along the coast of the peninsula, and dense green jungle reaches down to rocky headlands enclosing picturesque bays and sheltered sandy inlets. In times of peace and prosperity this palm-strewn land would be regarded as a tropical paradise, particularly

140

in the season from November to May when the sun shines all day, every day; the land becomes parched and the air is crisp, dry and invigorating. In the other six months, the rainy season, the rate of precipitation increases gradually, reaching a peak in July and August, when the climate is still hot but very humid. During this period spectacular thunderstorms accompany deluging rain which falls in tropical intensity, for hours on end, turning the storm drains into raging torrents.

Prior to my arrival in May 1968 a coup against the previous military government had restored a civil administration under Mr Siaka Stevens, the Prime Minister. My predecessor, as part of his job, had established good and friendly working relations with the officers of the displaced regime. Because his association with the overthrown military government had been so close, the army staff under the new administration tended to keep me at arm's length. Gradually, however, they accepted me, and the Force Commander, Brigadier John Bangura, with whom I had frequent, frank and useful discussions, became a firm friend to me and my family. Like the senior officers on his staff, he was Sandhurst trained and I was able to assist him in arranging courses for all ranks at military establishments in Britain, and in the purchase of appropriate equipment and materials for his troops. On several occasions the Brigadier invited me to accompany him on visits to his army bases throughout Sierra Leone. These gave me opportunities to see something of the country and the way of life of its people.


My upgrading to Commander came at last with this appointment. As I donned my new 'brass hat' my joy was doubled by the happiness it gave to my family who, like me, had feared that past events precluded any further advancement in the Service.

The two navy wives were much involved, particularly in the arrangements for social events both ashore and afloat. Visiting ships would inform us beforehand as to when they wished to entertain guests and how many were to be invited, then it was up to us to compile guest lists and get out the invitations.

We made arrangements for recreational trips for the ships' companies. The superb beaches with safe swimming offered great opportunities for all, and many residents from a large community of expatriates offered generous hospitality to officers and ratings.

The ships themselves reciprocated by giving parties aboard for both adults and children.

The world's largest countries were represented by embassies in Sierra Leone and the diplomatic circuit in the capital made for a busy social round. Sally fitted like a glove into this world and made many friends in the international community. She was a tower of strength, too, in fulfilling our need to offer entertainment not only to visiting ships, but also to the local army, and expatriate residents.

From their boarding schools in England Christopher and George flew out for the holidays. The British Caledonian aircraft, nicknamed 'Lollipop Specials', landed at Lungi airport and disgorged a full load of smiling and excited children. A social life of unlimited swimming, boating, sporting activities and partying lay before them, and I believe that memories of those days still loom large in their thoughts.

As a two-man band, my Chief Petty Officer Writer and I comprised the naval element on the High Commissioner's staff. For the greater part of my four-year tour I was fortunate to have CPO Stan Colley as my assistant. He was a smart, personable character; he and his wife were well liked in the community and made many friends. Apart from keeping our accounts and paying the crew of our launch and my driver, he arranged for the provision to our ships of all their requirements for fuel, water, mail, fresh vegetables and fruit and, of course, transport for shore leave and recreation. There was little that he could not organise. When ships stayed with us for several days there were always unforeseen matters to be dealt with. He took all these in his stride, and his multitude of contacts amongst the local population were of great value.

We maintained our own oiling jetty where warships and Royal Fleet Auxiliaries could take on fuel and water, but we had no manpower to help in getting the vessels alongside. For this we relied upon the Sierra Leone Ports Authority to provide us with a berthing party. Those who know West Africa will not be surprised to learn that, quite frequently, the berthing party which had been ordered did not turn up. On those occasions Stan Colley and I, dressed in our best white uniforms to welcome the visiting ship, were obliged to do the berthing ourselves. By the time we had taken the lines and secured the heavy, greasy steel hawsers to the bollards we were a sorry sight in our blackened clothes and shoes.

Nevertheless it did, I believe, give a lot of pleasure to the sailors watching from the deck, who obviously enjoyed the spectacle of a Commander and a Chief Petty Officer doing a bit of dirty work for a change.

On one occasion the bus taking a full load of sailors on a scenic tour of the jungle-clad peninsula broke down some distance from Freetown. For a locally hired bus to break down was not an occurrence that could be called exceptional, but this time it was unusual because it happened right outside a local bar. The wait for a relief vehicle was a long one and, whilst the afternoon wore on, and since the sailors were not short of money, the publican did a roaring trade. Inevitably an altercation arose, some passing citizen was struck by a flying bottle, the police were called and the entire busload of sailors was carted off to jail. The ship was sailing that evening and when the Captain found himself short of some 50 men he was, to put it kindly, not pleased. When I explained to him what had happened, and as his frustration and displeasure grew, I had recourse to the time-honoured solution to insurmountable problems. I turned to Stan Colley and said 'Chief – Get them out of jail!'

I did not delve too deeply into how he did it but, in time for sailing, the ship's company was once again complete, the Captain's mood improved and I had confirmed what I already knew – when you want something done well, and quickly, get the 'Chief' to do it.


One of our hydrographic ships, HMS *Hydra*, spent the greater part of a year making a survey of the Jong river in the south of Sierra Leone, and the adjacent coastal areas. The Sierra Leone government was considering the establishment of an extensive oil palm plantation in the southern part of the country. They requested the help of the Royal Navy in examining the feasibility of using the Jong river as a means of transporting the produce from the plantation to a point downstream where it could be transhipped from barges into ocean-going vessels. Using small boats, the surveyors spent long weeks in malaria infested jungle as they appraised the navigability of the upper reaches of the river.

From time to time *Hydra* spent days in Freetown. We got to know the Captain, Commander Bob Nesbitt, his officers and the

143

ship's company well and they became our friends. We were sorry to see them go when, after months of work in our area, they sailed for home. Their report, which we received in due course and handed to the Sierra Leone government, concluded that the river was navigable for the types of vessel needed. After all *Hydra*'s work, often in difficult and unhealthy conditions, I had hoped to find that the oil palm plantation project was to go ahead but nothing materialised in my time.

Our 54-four foot launch, *Tagarin*, had been on station in Freetown for 25 years. Driven by a powerful Perkins diesel engine, she was manned by a crew of four: coxswain, engineer and two seaman deckhands. When our ships were at anchor in Freetown roads, *Tagarin* was busily occupied moving supplies and catering for the many needs of a vessel offshore. As the naval workboat in Sierra Leone since 1943, she must have tended thousands of our ships and, after all this time in tropical waters, she needed constant attention, chiefly in combating the dreaded toredo worm which was doing its evil work within the timbers of the hull, even beneath the copper sheathing. Despite her age she was our pride and joy and, accordingly, our aim was to keep her in smart and sparkling appearance. This was enthusiastically undertaken by her dedicated crew.

As well as attending to the many needs of our warships, *Tagarin*'s services were in regular demand by the High Commission for transporting staff, families, visitors and mail to and from the international airport at Lungi, which lay on the northern shore of the five-mile-wide harbour. With so many ships calling, we had few free weekends but, when we did, *Tagarin* came into her own for deep-sea fishing. The sea off Sierra Leone enjoyed an abundance of barracuda and large mackerel which, when we were lucky, were ready takers of our spinners and plugs. Christopher, our elder son, was our master angler. Given the rod when nobody else could get a bite, he could be relied upon to hook a fish in quick time. His record catch was a 35-pound barracuda. Bigger and more menacing monsters of the deep were often near the boat, usually the grotesque hammerhead sharks and, once, schools of killer whales.

Peter Scott, who managed the British American Tobacco Company, owned his own high-speed motor boat. We had much in common

144

as he had been a wartime Fleet Air Arm fighter pilot, and on many occasions we joined him for a fast and exhilarating trip out to the Banana Islands, some 20 miles offshore. A favourite resort for those who had the means to get there, these islands offered sheltered bays with wonderful opportunities for snorkelling or just luxuriating in the warm clear water. All sorts of fish, including rays, moray eels and groupers, were to be seen and, for the adventurous, caught with spear-guns. For barbecues on the beach or in the boat the red snapper was prized above all others for its superlative flavour.

In the Sierra Leone river some 20 miles north-east of Freetown lies the former slave station of Bunce Island. With a circumference of one mile, it contains the ruins of the fort where slaves were collected and held in captivity until they were taken in chains aboard the ships which would transport them to the New World. The tangle of creepers and the dense vegetation that now engulf the decaying dungeons cannot hide the sinister atmosphere that hangs heavy over the island.

Musket balls and multi-coloured beads of assorted shapes and sizes were everywhere to be found scattered on the sandy beaches of this roughly circular island. Lying in the midst of the steamy tropical river, the jungle seemed usually to be airless. An exploration of the ruins and a walk round the shoreline made for a sweltering, sweat-soaked experience, but such physical discomfort was outweighed by the evil fascination of this menacing and historic place. An excursion up-river to Bunce Island was an adventure enjoyed by many of our friends in Freetown and by short-stay visitors from abroad, when *Tagarin*'s wide decks and spacious cabin would give comfort and refreshing breezes to our passengers as we made our way back to the capital.


Close liaison with the Sierra Leone Army was an important element of my work and this gave me many opportunities for travel throughout the country. To maintain strong links with Britain, officers and soldiers undertook courses in the UK. Parade ground drill was immaculate and followed the standards and traditions of the former colonial era. The band, whose musicians were trained at the British Military School of Music, and whose repertoire consisted of all the well-known British marches, was of high quality.

Although Sierra Leone had been independent for seven years,

the strains of a developing nation were very evident, with tribal influences strong and deep-rooted. The government was both wary of the army's loyalty and, at the same time, largely dependent upon it for maintaining power. However, the army was unable to keep out of political involvement, and a number of officers and men, including the Force Commander, suffered the most tragic consequences during my tour.

Sierra Leone recognised the Nationalist Chinese as the government of China and the Taiwanese authorities gave aid to Sierra Leone, particularly in the field of agriculture. Although there was no starvation in the country, malnutrition was widespread. Cassava was the staple food but a balanced diet was absent. Three demonstration farms were developed by the Nationalists, one on the outskirts of Freetown. Land was cleared and, under the matchless traditional skill of the Chinese farmers, soil that was generally regarded as close to infertile produced an astonishing abundance of vegetables and fruit of superb quality and variety, in all seasons. The beautifully laid out farm attracted expatriates for much of their fresh provisions. What better form of international aid could there be? In the last year of my tour the Sierra Leone government decided to recognise Communist China instead of the Nationalists as the legitimate government of China, so the Ambassador and his staff from Taiwan left the country, together with the farmers from the three developments.

It very quickly became apparent that the techniques so carefully demonstrated to the Sierra Leoneans had not even crossed the boundaries of the farm to the land of the Africans living round it. This was another example of the near impossibility of changing the ingrained habits and traditions of ordinary people.

The farm died and, in three months, the jungle had overwhelmed it. It might never have been there. I wept.

The new representatives of China duly arrived and, to celebrate their installation into the diplomatic community of Sierra Leone, they gave a reception sporting a truly splendid buffet of their national dishes. Sally and I were tucking into this delicious food, always a favourite of ours, when the new Chinese Minister came over to speak to us. Savouring a spring roll, I complimented him upon the excellence of the buffet and explained that both my wife and I were very fond of Chinese food. He replied, 'The

Chinese people express their solidarity with the people of Great Britain.'

I then commented upon the fact that in almost every town in Britain there is a Chinese restaurant and I suggested that perhaps English restaurants would be almost unknown in China. He replied, 'The people of China are so grateful to the people of Great Britain for supporting their entry into the United Nations.'

Next I informed our host that Peking Duck was our favourite dish. I was wearing my best white uniform for the occasion and he replied, 'The Chinese people are so favourably disposed towards the Royal Navy.' Thinking of HMS *Amethyst* and choking on a king prawn, I felt unable to pursue the conversation further. Sally took up the challenge, however, by expressing the hope that he and his staff would enjoy their stay in Sierra Leone. He replied, 'We are very happy to be here now that the imperialists and colonialists have gone.'

For me this was a memorable feast.

My first High Commissioner was Mr Stanley Fingland (now Sir Stanley). When his tour was completed he was followed by Mr Stephen Olver (now Sir Stephen). As I got to know them it was clear to me why they had reached the rank and position they held. I always admired the calm and clearheaded way in which they handled difficult situations, whether political or operational, not a few of which originated in my department, usually when movements of our ships caused political embarrassment. I was fortunate in my two 'bosses', especially Stephen Olver, whom I got to know well. He gave me great support, and I remember him with admiration and affection.

Since Independence, and for most of my time in the country, Sierra Leone had recognised our Queen as head of state. Shortly before I left in 1972, however, the Sierra Leone government decided to declare the country a republic. The Prime Minister, Siaka Stevens, was to become the first President.

At a splendid ceremony in the great stadium the armed forces, civilian groups of all kinds and government organisations took part in glittering and colourful events. The army, as always, displayed its superb drill in immaculate uniforms. The finale of the day was a grand march-past to salute the President of the new Republic. At this moment ties to the British Crown were severed.

As the army band led the march past the rostrum the big drum thumped out the time to that rousing and most magnificent of all marching tunes:

di DUM di DUM di DUM di di DUM
di di DUM DUM di di di di DUM...

It was none other than 'The British Grenadiers'. How could one fail to be charmed by such delightful innocence and such simple guilelessness?

How fortunate we were to live for four years in Sierra Leone in those days when all the good things of life were available. How happily we recall our African staff, including the crew of our launch *Tagarin*: Johnson, the coxswain; Koroma, the engineer and Johnny Kamara, the No. 1 deckhand. What affectionate memories we have of Martin, our driver, who shepherded our whole family with wonderful reliability and friendliness and, after his retirement, our smart new driver, Manna. In the house we were fortunate indeed to enjoy the services of Mansaray, our houseboy, and of Saidu, our cook. All these became our close friends, from whom we parted with sadness when our tour ended in 1972 and we sailed away in the Elder Dempster liner *Aureol* to return to Britain.

*Chapter 19*

# Finale (1974)

*And to make an end is to make a beginning.*
*The end is where we start from* – T.S. Eliot

My next appointment was to the Ministry of Defence as Area Officer to the Sea Cadet Corps in the Greater London Area. The Area comprised 60 units of the Corps. The cadets were encouraged to make progress in sports and adventurous activities as well as in nautical subjects. With a background of discipline they learnt to work as a team and to develop qualities of self-assurance and leadership. Although the units varied greatly, many compared favourably with regular naval training establishments. I was very impressed by what I saw of the much-criticised youngsters of the day, and by the dedicated staff who gave so much of their time and effort to run the units.

During this period Christopher flew off to Australia to make his way from scratch in a new country. We were delighted at how, by his own efforts, he made a success of his life in a strange land. George passed his 'A' Levels and, after leaving school, spent a year working partly in Canada and partly in the South of France. With this valuable experience of the real world behind him, he went off to university, to emerge three years later with graduation and a BSc. We watched all this with pride in our two boys.

The day of my retirement from the Royal Navy after 33 years' service dawned on 5th September 1974. At Portsmouth Barracks I completed the final steps which were to turn me once again into a civilian. As I visited the departments and lunched in the wardroom, wearing my uniform for the last time, I was struck by an overwhelming sense of sadness. Only on that day did I become fully aware that the life which had given me so many adventures, a share of triumphs, disasters, failures, successes and such absorbing endeavours, was to end by putting my signature to a few pieces of paper.

With the handing-in of my identity card I ceased to be a member of the 'club' and I left for home with a heavy heart. Soon, however, I embarked upon the search for a new way of life. This came with my appointment as Land Agent to a large agricultural company. Having pursued my first career on the sea and in the air, it seemed appropriate to complete my working days on the land.

Dramatic and rapid changes in all aspects of aviation took place in my time. From piston-engined aircraft to pure jets and to turbo-props; from subsonic flight to supersonic; from aircraft with tailwheels to those with tricycle undercarriages; from fixed-wing craft to helicopters; from conventional to vertical take-off and landing.

In the operation of aircraft from carriers huge improvements were made – notably by the angled deck design, and by the mirror landing sight. These alone made deck landing much less hazardous. With jet propulsion it was possible to design aircraft with good forward vision for the pilot on the approach and this, too, made for much safer arrivals on deck.

From my early days, when we set off with a map, a dead-reckoning plan and a rudimentary weather forecast, we progressed to total air control from the ground with reliable aids to monitor the plane's movements and to bring the pilot to a safe landing in all weathers. The high-altitude performance of aircraft now allows us to fly above the weather instead of under it or through it.

Progress in the future will be as rapid and fundamental as in the past 50 years. Those entering the Service now will experience equally remarkable developments during their flying careers. Only the dreamers can foretell what they may be.

Looking back on my time in the Navy I recall most of all the good fellowship that characterised every squadron and ship in which I served, the fun we had and the hazards shared. Like all aviators, I mourn the loss of many friends and colleagues, several of whom had been my cabin mates. Their unfailing cheerfulness, their light-hearted courage and their final sacrifice will ever be recognised and remembered by those who serve, or will serve, in the Fleet Air Arm.

# *Appendix A*

By: Lieutenant Commander A.I.R. Shaw, MBE, Royal Navy
Spring 1966

### The Fleet Air Arm: Out of Sight – Out of Mind

Great controversy has been aroused in aviation circles and in the armed services by the government's decision to dispense with the Navy's aircraft carriers. The controversy has been restricted largely to these professional bodies and has not appeared to touch the general public of this country. This must seem strange to the men of the Fleet Air Arm but it is the logical outcome of a silent service tradition. The policy of silence has resulted in a deep and widespread ignorance of British naval aviation in all sections of the community, extending to Members of Parliament and even to some Ministers of the Crown.

In this article an attempt is made to look at the role of the Fleet Air Arm since the critical years of the Second World War and to give the reader some facts on which to base his judgement of recent defence policy decisions.

Our study can usefully begin in 1941, when many of our towns and cities lay in ruins. These devastated areas in our midst were symptomatic of the plight of Britain and our war effort as a whole. In every field our fortunes were at a low ebb and, far from showing any hopeful signs of improvement, they were deteriorating. On land we knew of little but retreat, and in the air we lacked the means to retaliate. This was bad enough, but it was in the Atlantic that we saw our situation to be truly desperate. Our shipping losses were staggering and they were fast draining away our capacity to survive, let alone to fight back. Of the Battle of the Atlantic at that time Winston Churchill wrote:

> Amid the torrent of violent events one anxiety reigned supreme, battles might be won or lost, enterprises might succeed or miscarry, territory might be gained or quitted, but dominating all our power to carry on the war, or even to keep ourselves alive, lay our mastery of the ocean routes and the free approach and entry to our ports. The only thing that ever really frightened me during the war was the U-boat peril.

Of the enormous menace of the submarine and of the insupportable losses which our shipping was sustaining in the Atlantic in early 1941 he wrote later:

> Indeed, it was to me almost a relief to turn from these deadly under-tides to the ill-starred but spirited enterprises in the military sphere. How willingly would I have exchanged a full scale attempt at invasion for this shapeless, measureless peril...

Our convoys of merchantmen and their escorts operated without effective air support and some measure of the seriousness with which we viewed the appalling threat of the U-boats, and their associated long-range reconnaissance planes, can be gauged by a look at the countermeasures which we were driven to adopt. One of these was the conversion of some vessels into CAM (Catapult-armed Merchantmen) ships with their lone Hurricane fighter. In the history of warfare this surely was the most un-British weapon system ever openly to have been used by our regular forces, employing tactics which must be ranked as approaching in desperation those of the Japanese Kamikaze. The employment of this defensive system did, however, show that the lesson of the need for air-power at sea had been learnt; and it was with great good fortune that we found that it had been learnt no less well in the United States of America. For, since many of the supplies which failed to survive the Atlantic crossing to Britain came from her own factories and farms, it was a bitter experience for Americans to see the consequences of our impotence in the fight against the submarine.

But it was not only in the Atlantic that the Americans had been watching events at sea with the closest interest. They had noted, too, that the crucial importance of naval air power had been dramatically demonstrated in the Mediterranean at the battle of Taranto. An outline of this historical action is worth a few moments' study.

In the latter half of 1940 the Royal Navy's strength was thinly spread and a large part of our fleet, which was so sorely needed in the Atlantic, was required in the Mediterranean to counter the threat of the Italian Navy. Despite numerous offensive sweeps throughout the central Mediterranean by the British fleet, the major part of the Italian Navy had still not been brought to any decisive action. It remained elusive, intact and a constant threat to British operations.

In late October 1940, at the time of Italy's attack on Greece, Mussolini's fleet was found by air reconnaissance to be in the apparently secure port of Taranto, the finest naval base in Italy. Because of its natural shape, and its construction, the harbour was a safe refuge against any form of surface or submarine attack. Against possible air attack the Italians had taken every precaution and the ships in harbour were protected by the most comprehensive defences.

With the arrival in the Mediterranean of the aircraft carrier *Illustrious* the prospect of a naval air attack on ships in Taranto became a practical possibility. Her aircrews were trained in the type of night torpedo attack which would be required to penetrate such formidable defences.

After a short planning period, during which an additional Italian battleship arrived in the harbour, the attack was delivered on the night of 11th/12th November. The results of the battle more than justified the greatest hopes of all its planners. For at the cost of two aircraft and four officers, two of whom happily survived as prisoners of war, half of the Italian battlefleet had been put out of action; one battleship lay on the bottom and two others were beached in a sinking condition. Several other ships were damaged.

The handful of officers who flew their slow and lumbering Swordfish through the night of 11th November 1940 had inflicted more damage on the enemy in one hour than 150 warships had inflicted on the Germans in two days at the Battle of Jutland. They had altered completely the balance of power in the Mediterranean, and effected as radical a change in the strategical conditions in

European waters as the Japanese carriers at Pearl Harbour and the American carriers at Midway were to do in the Pacific more than a year later.

The success of the attack was of the greatest significance for the future. It demonstrated to the whole world, and even to many detractors and doubters within the Royal Navy itself, the potentiality of the aircraft carriers. For the first time the carrier was shown to be not merely an indispensable component of a modern fleet, but a mobile airfield capable of operating aircraft against objectives otherwise immune to attack.

The achievement of the naval aircraft at Taranto, plus the awareness that Britain's desperate situation in the Atlantic was due to a lack of seaborne air power, led directly to a technical revolution in the shipyards of America. Backed by a vast organisation, the production of escort carriers for the US Navy, and for lease-lend to Britain, was begun. But, sadly, even the massive industrial power of America could not build and launch carriers overnight and so, for another year at least, our shipping losses continued to mount.

In early 1942 these ships began to roll down the slipways, and by the end of that year the new generation of escort carriers was coming into service in numbers that can justly be described as miraculous. So fast were they built and commissioned that within two years some 58 escort carriers and MAC (Merchant aircraft carriers) ships were operational with the British fleet alone. In addition, our force of large fleet carriers was growing steadily in number. In these days of limited defence budgets one can only marvel at the total number of aircraft carriers, both British and American, which were manned and thrown into war against the U-boat. Here, at last, we saw the Royal Navy, through the use of air power, fulfilling satisfactorily its classic role as the protector of our sea communications, the prime task for which our navy has always existed.

Results were quickly apparent and by mid-1943 the crisis in the Atlantic was over. U-boat losses were mounting but, best of all, because they were forced to remain submerged, they were more and more often unable to position themselves for attacks on our convoys.

With our sea lanes secured, the Fleet Air Arm was able to go over to the offensive on an ever-increasing scale, playing a major role in all the big amphibious operations throughout the Mediterranean.

When the war in Europe ended, our carriers sailed to the Far East to join the mighty naval forces of the USA in the vast campaign across the Pacific Ocean to the homeland of Japan. A long struggle which, from the beginning, had been based squarely upon the mobility and concentrated power of the aircraft carrier.

It was the pattern of the Second World War which forced the evolution of the Fleet Air Arm. Its development was rapid, despite the reluctance of other departments and of a large and influential part of the Navy itself. For Britain and America alike, naval aviation progressed from an untried and often distrusted weapon to the prime instrument of maritime power. Its evolution could not be stifled because our bitter and tragic experiences without it had been too painful to brook of partisanship. The Fleet Air Arm had evolved through our desperate need and it emerged in the classic role as defender of Britain's sea communications and, in the end, as our foremost offensive weapon.

*The past 20 years*

The experiences of the past 20 years have confirmed the position which had been reached by the end of the war; namely, that naval air power is the chief requirement of a maritime nation. The relative decline of Britain as a world power has made us no less reliant upon ships to maintain the trade on which our standard of living depends. We are as much a maritime nation as ever, and the very decline of our power tends to put temptation in the way of any nation wishing to hit us where it hurts most, by jeopardising our trade or the stability upon which it rests.

There has been no lack of incidents to test Britain's resolution and capacity to defend our vital interests, and any study of the course of these affairs shows that it is upon the Fleet Air Arm that our governments have depended for the quick response which has so often been crucial. The study will show clearly that the branches of the British Services which have contributed to the resolution of the emergency situations since the war have been the Royal Marine Commandos, the Transport Command of the Royal Air Force, certain units of the Army, and the Fleet Air Arm. These are the forces which have done the bulk of the fighting when it has broken out, or which have provided the threat of military action which has so often been sufficient to prevent any fighting from starting.

As is proper in time of peace, and especially since the danger of escalation to nuclear war has been apparent, our first interest has been to prevent trouble from breaking out in areas where peace has been at risk. Examples of the employment of naval aviation in this role were seen during the threatened attack upon Kuwait by Iraq in 1961, and the suppression of the East African mutinies in early 1964.

When Britain received the call for help from Kuwait to counter the open threat from the revolutionary regime in Iraq, it was within 24 hours that the Royal Marines of No. 42 Commando were being put ashore from the carrier *Bulwark*. A few days later the carrier *Victorious* arrived to take over the entire responsibility for air defence. As a result of this timely assistance the threatened Iraqi invasion was averted and not a single soldier crossed the border.

The army mutinies in East Africa followed upon the revolution in Zanzibar of January 1964 and Britain was called upon to help in their suppression by the newly independent government of Tanganyika. The required aid was immediately forthcoming as No. 45 Royal Marine Commando was landed from the carrier *Centaur*, which then put to sea to cover their operations with her aircraft. Combined assaults involving the Commandos, RAF Transport Command and the Fleet Air Arm's fighters, sometimes giving cover as much as 400 miles inland, brought the emergency to an end within four days. In Parliament, on 27th January, the then Secretary of State for Commonwealth Relations, Mr Duncan Sandys, read out a letter from President Nyereri to the House, in which the President expressed his gratitude for the prompt action taken by Her Majesty's Government on his request, and the magnificent way in which the operation was carried out by all concerned.

In each of these cases the carrier force was on the spot within hours of our receiving the call for assistance, and the very fact of its presence was enough to prevent violence from breaking out.

The well-known offshore islands of China, Quemoy and Matsu present another interesting example of the deterrent effect of naval air power. On the very doorstep of Communist China, but still occupied by Nationalist forces, these islands have been guaranteed by the USA as part of the blanket assurance to Chiang Kai-shek's island of Formosa. So close are they to China that they are accustomed to regular shelling by artillery from the mainland, and they obviously exist as a constant and galling humiliation to the government of the most populous nation on earth. Preparations by China to occupy these islands have consequently been made on several occasions but, each time, the US Government has moved its carriers into the area and it is significant that no invasion has yet been attempted.

Some examples have been given of the way in which carrier forces have successfully kept the peace on behalf of their governments but, unfortunately, threatened trouble does from time to time break out into actual warfare and, in such cases, it is our immediate and urgent responsibility to prevent the fighting from growing into a major conflict. There have been several instances of such emergencies since the Second World War. The first was the Malayan Communist insurrection which began in 1947.

For the latter part of this ten-year emergency, in which new techniques of subversion were employed by the enemy and against which new countermeasures had to be devised and adopted, the Fleet Air Arm played its part. It was during this period that they pioneered the use of helicopters in support of our troops in the jungle, and the extent to which this has become accepted form in modern warfare is very apparent today in Vietnam.

The confrontation of Malaysia by Indonesia may now be over but, for four years, it was a very real war in the Far East and, in that time, it was the chief preoccupation of our carrier forces. The war was finally abandoned by Indonesia despite Dr Sukarno's boast, in 1964, that before the cock crowed on New Year's Day 1965 he would have crushed Malaysia, and despite the fact that, to back up his claim, he sent his forces not only across the border in Borneo but landed them from the sea and parachuted them from the air on the mainland of Malaya itself. The helicopters from our carriers were disembarked for long periods in the Borneo jungle, where they supported the troops and aided the local population. The carriers themselves were almost invariably in the area, and their presence was a constant reminder to Sukarno that his homeland was not immune to retaliation if he overstepped the mark in his aggression against Malaysia.

Some cases have been quoted to illustrate the use of carriers in the rapid deployment of force to prevent trouble starting, or from spreading into major conflicts. The experiences of the United States Navy have been similar to ours and the Chief of Naval Operations wrote, in 1965:

157

In some 15 Cold War incidents since Korea ... the seapower factors of mobility, flexibility and responsiveness were used by the Navy in almost a classic sense as, in incident after incident, Naval forces just happened to appear on the scene at the proper time and in the proper amounts. When these Naval forces arrive in distant disturbed areas they are fully prepared for either conversation or conflict.

It is unfortunately impossible, however, always to contain the outbreak of hostilities and so prevent the onset of major wars, and there have been several large-scale conflicts since 1945 in which Britain has been directly involved, and others in which America has operated without us, as at present in Vietnam. In each of these conflicts naval aviation has played a major role, and in each one the peace of the world as a whole has been threatened. I refer in particular to Korea, Suez, Cuba and Vietnam.

Because the Korean War took place on the other side of the world it is perhaps not generally realised in this country that for over three years it surpassed in horror anything that has been experienced by Britain in modern times. The bulk of the United Nations forces were, of course, supplied by the United States but Britain, too, played her part with the provision of ground forces and naval forces. Her air power came exclusively from the Fleet Air Arm. Who has not heard of the glorious Glosters or read of their heroic exploits, or those of the Royal Marines who fought alongside them? Few, perhaps, remember that Fleet Air Arm aircraft were in action within five days of the North Korean invasion of the South, and that they, and the carriers from which they operated, were there almost without a break for the next three years. Five British carriers, with 16 naval air squadrons, served there during the period and over 29,800 operational sorties were flown by their aircrew, a number of whom did not return.

For those with eyes to see, the Korean War established once and for all that the aircraft carrier was the ideal means of deploying air power. It operated from an environment uninhibited by international politics. It was independent of the army ashore, requiring neither their protection nor a share of their available communications and supplies, and yet its mobility offered them the most immediate response to their calls for assistance. These lessons were not lost upon the military planners of the United States and, since Korea,

158

a large force of powerful ships has emerged carrying aircraft of the very highest performance. It is significant that in this, the greatest struggle which has occurred in the last 20 years, it was exclusively upon the Fleet Air Arm that Britain relied to provide the air support which the United Nations, and our own ground forces within it, so desperately needed.

The war of Suez again illustrated the reliance which British Governments have consistently placed on the Fleet Air Arm. For, if ever there was a war overseas where the area of combat was within the range of our shore-based aircraft, this was it. And yet it was upon the carrier aircraft that our forces depended for by far the greater part of the offensive sorties flown. The three carriers *Eagle*, *Albion* and *Bulwark* flew some 1,600 sorties between them, while 400 others were made by aircraft from the helicopter carriers *Ocean* and *Theseus*. Military history was again made by our naval aircraft when, on 6th November 1956, No. 45 Royal Marine Commando was landed in the first amphibious assault ever made by helicopters.

As a result of their experiences since 1944, the men of the Fleet Air Arm have grown accustomed to finding themselves the first to be called whenever Britain is involved in an emergency. The call has come in almost every case, whether it has been threatened trouble; or small-scale fighting requiring the promptest action to prevent it from growing; or major warfare such as in Korea or Suez.

Our carriers played a predominant part in maintaining the oil embargo off Mozambique. That they operated with no international embarrassment, and with no publicity, for the most prolonged periods at sea in the history of British carriers in peacetime, is a measure of the worth of this method of deploying air power. The very fact that our carriers are able to operate in isolation from the vagaries of local and international politics is one of the chief assets that they offer to any British Government, but it is largely for the same reason that this force, called upon by Britain in her every hour of need, has carried out its tasks unsung and often unrecognised by the greater part of the British public. How, otherwise, could our carrier force be threatened with oblivion with scarcely a murmur of dissent from the electorate?

'Out of sight – out of mind' is one of naval aviation's greatest advantages when it is operating in protection of our vital interests overseas, but it is its greatest weakness when defending itself against political attack.

In this article an attempt has been made to outline the development of the Fleet Air Arm from the middle year of World War Two, but it has given mention to only some of the incidents in which it has been involved. An effort has been made to spotlight those branches of Britain's forces which have contributed most to the active support of British interests overseas, and to the suppression of violence when this has been necessary. The most active of these forces, the Fleet Air Arm, is now threatened with extinction for lack of knowledge of its past and its capabilities for the future. If this threat should be fulfilled Britain will cease to be an effective maritime power, but her position as a maritime nation will remain. However rich, or however poor, we become, whether we go into Europe or stay outside, we will be dependent upon ships and a stable world for the trade and the goods on which we live, and without which we die.

Over the past 400 years we have learnt time after time that, as a maritime nation, we must be a maritime power. Let us not now discard this versatile branch of the service which has so emphatically proved its value. For, once thrown away, it could not be revived in a generation.

# *Appendix B*

During my flying career I logged 4,568 flying hours.
I baled out once
I ditched once

My total of 610 deck landings comprised:
  534 deck landings by day
   72 deck landings by night
    4 landings on the rubber deck

From my log book I list the aircraft I have flown as first pilot:

N3N3/Stearman
Kingfisher
Harvard
Buffalo
Piper Cub
Master
Tiger Moth
Proctor
Prentice
Oxford
Dominie
Anson
Devon
Hurricane
Spitfire/Seafire (numerous marques)
Fulmar
Wildcat
Firefly (numerous marques)
Sea Fury
Firebrand
Swordfish
Mamba Balliol
Reliant
Balliol
Vampire
Meteor
Attacker
Viking
Valletta
Supermarine 508

Varsity
Lancaster
Lincoln
Tomtit
Chipmunk
Mosquito
Seahawk
Sea Prince
Provost
Sea Venom
Canberra
Avro 707
Gannet
N7/46
Avenger
Wyvern
Hunter
Seamew
Brigand
Shooting Star
FJ3 Fury
F9F8 Cougar
AD5N Skyraider
SNB Expediter
F2H Banshee
F3D Skynight
F3H Demon
F4D Skyray
Sea Vixen

Hiller
Whirlwind (several marques)
P 531
Dragonfly

# Index

163